Backyard Beekeeping
and Honey Production

Backyard Beekeeping and Honey Production

Phil Rant

THE CROWOOD PRESS

First published in 2011 by
The Crowood Press Ltd
Ramsbury, Marlborough
Wiltshire SN8 2HR

www.crowood.com

British Library Cataloguing-in-Publication Data
A catalogue record for this book is available from the British Library.

ISBN 978 1 84797 268 2

Frontispiece: Cells showing larvae at later growth stages.
(Courtesy Rupert Stephenson.)

Illustrations by Caroline Pratt

Disclaimer
The author and publisher do not accept any responsibility in any manner
whatsoever for any error or omission, or any loss, damage, injury, adverse
outcome, or liability of any kind incurred as a result of the use of any of the
information contained in this book, or reliance upon it.

Typeset by Jean Cussons Typesetting, Diss, Norfolk

Printed and bound in Singapore by Craft Print International

CONTENTS

ACKNOWLEDGEMENTS

In writing a book of this nature, I am constantly reminded of my limitations. It is only when you need to explain things to others that you discover them, even to the extent in my case of being unfamiliar with the machinations of the modern computer. So, for the benefit of all those whom I have annoyed over the past months with my seemingly stupid questions, I must now record my sincere and heartfelt thanks.

To all the bee inspectors I ever met for their humour and wise advice that I have attempted to follow, take a bow, you are the unsung heroes of the beekeeping brotherhood.

To Claire Waring, editor of *Bee Craft*, for permission to refer to an article published in that great magazine.

To Gill Smith, Sales Director of Thorne's Beehive Equipment at Wragby; in the middle of their busiest season ever, she took the time and trouble to forward a number of the images reproduced in this work – thank you.

To Jenna Cook and the principal photographer David Crossley at The Food and Environment Research Agency, my thanks for permitting the use of the superb images of bee ailments and for putting me on the right road when I strayed.

To my Honorary Research Assistant, Roger Morris, for all the time and trouble taken by him to attempt to translate my needs, in showering me with more research than I will ever require and tolerating my responses when he did so. After helping me with four books he must now have the skin of a rhinoceros!

To the Lovely Cabbage Dragon, and she knows who she is, for making an offer she probably regrets: that of compiling the index for this tome, a very sincere thank you.

To Rupert Stephenson for permission to use a number of the images from his apparently inexhaustible collection, and to others who unknowingly provided some of the images used by the author.

Last, but (as they say) by no means least, to my good friend and fellow author, J.C. Jeremy Hobson, who after jointly writing some books with me (or more accurately, the other way round) still had the humility to permit me to claim that this one was all my own work and without whose guidance and persistent encouragement it would never have been completed.

INTRODUCTION

The main purpose of this little book is to encourage and advise those who are about to take up this most fascinating of hobbies, and perhaps it may offer some help to those who have already begun. It is true that we never stop learning; or rather we should not do so. However, the scope of this book is not large enough to contain all the information you may desire, and it is doubtful any single book could do so. Accordingly, one of the first pieces of advice I can offer is for you to read extensively; beg, buy or borrow the books, from libraries, or from friends, wherever you can discover information, and there is of course the Internet.

However, be very careful: eventually you may conclude that personal experience counts for a lot, that there are many wrong ways of doing things but, strangely, a number of right ones, all apparently equally effective. It is in this frame of mind that this book is written. I have attempted to ensure that nothing I have written is incorrect but I hope you will forgive me for any errors I have made – even at my advanced age, I am still learning, and that is something that makes beekeeping such a fascinating subject.

Little did I suspect when I first became addicted to the life of the honey bee that over half a century later I would be attempting to write such a book, but I am motivated by the desire to pass on some ideas, and hope that I can pass on my love of the creature.

I hope that the reader will prosper and learn and in time perhaps will have much to contribute to the furtherance of knowledge.

The sum total of information regarding the keeping of bees did not all come from the scientific community: much has emerged from the ordinary (if you will excuse the word) beekeeper, who has taken the time and trouble to record his or her observations – the beekeeper who has not been afraid to experiment with new systems of management and has passed on this information for future generations.

You will, in the course of time, read many books and articles on the subject, and some may appear to contradict others. However, you will soon discover that the authors of the respective articles have written of something that works for them, and they are all correct.

The most important consideration before you choose to begin is that we are dealing with living creatures. They cannot be ignored because of your lifestyle; you must consider their needs before your own on occasions and, although not to the extent of, say, a dog or cat, they can be a tie. Having said that, if you embark on this journey, you will discover a truly rewarding relationship, you will learn to love and admire these hard-working and endearing insects. In doing so you may even learn something about yourself, for with bees, there is little room for impatience or bad temper; you must always handle them in a benevolent and gentle manner, always making plenty of time to do so, or suffer the consequence!

The traditional image of a beekeeper is most likely that of a male, probably of a certain age and with plenty of time to stand

and stare. It is true that there is little place in this hobby for excessive excitability and impatience but young people, especially children, can take to the hobby with only a little self-discipline and it must be remembered that the children are our future and the future of the bee.

In my humble opinion, many of the best amateur beekeepers are women. They have the patience and gentle benevolence that are required, are more likely to be open to learning and are certainly less aggressive. I often assisted a lovely lady to work her bees; she loved them but arthritis in the fingers had meant she was no longer confident in gripping the frames and feared she would hurt her beloved creatures. On such occasions, a few young bees would drop to the grass whilst I manipulated the frames for her, and she would immediately scoop them up with her bare hands and return them lovingly to the hive. It was also very noticeable that despite her infirmity, she was reluctant to give up caring for her bees. That is what I wish to pass on, that is what I would wish you to become.

Perhaps most importantly, consider your service to the bee. The creature is going through hard times and bee losses are being reported all over the globe. Over a third of our food depends almost entirely on the bee but agricultural sprays and the spread of disease, especially the Varroa mite, is decimating the world population. What is becoming clear is that the increasing number of colonies being kept in backyards by dedicated and enthusiastic amateurs may well hold the key to survival for these creatures while we sort out their problems. The rural environment has proved to be very successful for the bee, with less use of chemical sprays, access to a wealth of blossom in gardens and parks and above all the individual care from beekeepers possibly staving off a global disaster; I do hope so. The term 'beekeeper' is correct – you should aim to keep bees, do not expect the bees to keep you!

On that final note, if you have picked up this book mainly in the hope of making some money, please put it back on the shelf, now. But if, however, you wish to follow a wonderful hobby which, despite its pitfalls and disappointments, frequently brings a lot of pleasure (and now and then a 'taste of honey'), please read on, with a big 'thank you' from me and from the bees.

CHAPTER 1

THE HONEY BEE

It is not the objective of this chapter to explore in depth the biology of the honey bee, but rather to give some insight into this creature and the essential differences between it and close relatives such as the bumble bees, wasps and hornets.

The honey bee, *Apis millifera millifera* to give it its correct name (more frequently written as *Apis mellifera*), belongs to a group of insects that exist throughout the temperate zones of the world. The family is large and members vary in size and habitat, but the most important aspect of their lifestyle, to man at least, is that they make and store honey. In the process they provide probably the greatest service to man, that of pollinating our food crops. It is estimated that over one third of food required by mankind is dependent on bees and other pollinating insects and that bees are mainly responsible for £200 million of food production in the UK alone. It has been estimated that the bees from an active colony may pollinate three million flowers in a single day!

The disastrous losses of bees recorded in the winters of 2007 and 2008 were estimated at 30 per cent of the total population and significant government help has been provided in the form of research money to halt this decline. But the bees' search for the nectar provided by flowers to encourage their visits does not extend merely to food crops.

These busy creatures work high in the tree canopy to pollinate a multitude of trees, enabling them to produce seed to continue the generations, and the same bee can be seen in the lowland meadows at ground level pollinating the grasses and clovers that supply food for animals of all sizes.

Honey bee on borage flower. (Courtesy The Food and Environment Research Agency, Crown Copyright.)

Sharing genes

Charles Darwin was fascinated with bees and other communal insects such as ants and termites. The main aim of all life appeared to be to pass on their genes by reproduction. Why then should these creatures opt to sacrifice this opportunity to serve a single community? The answer seemed quite simple: as all members of the colony shared the same genes, in working together as a group they had a better chance of passing on more of their genes to future generations.

THE HONEY BEE AND ITS LIFESTYLE

The honey bee has a particular lifestyle: an individual bee cannot exist alone, and without the hive its lifespan is measured in hours. Only with constant contact with the queen and other members of the colony will it survive, so the hive is essential. (We use the term 'hive' to describe both the home that they live in, and the colony or community of bees that reside therein, which is perhaps a little confusing. In the following I am referring to the family group, community or colony, call it what you will.) At the centre of the hive is the queen, once more a bit of a misnomer, since although the hive cannot survive for long without the queen, she does not rule the hive. They will soon dispose of her, and replace her if she does not come up with the goods!

The queen

This is, or should be, the only fertile female within the colony. She is essentially an egg-laying machine; having previously flown from the hive and mated with one or more drones (of which more later) she will return to a life of constant egg-laying and, apart from swarming when necessary, may never fly again. She is capable of working for perhaps five years or more, but the normal working life is two or three years.

Her every need will be provided by the mass of workers surrounding her. Observe the queen in the hive and you will notice a number of workers constantly grooming or caressing her. Some will be cleaning her; others will offer her food; still others will be guiding her into cleaned and empty cells to deposit her eggs. But the act of cleaning and caressing her is not an act of worship. A fecund and active queen will exude a creamy fluid, often referred to as the 'queen sub-stance'. This is passed on from one bee to another, and its strength and volume ensures that all members of the hive are aware of her active nature and that the hive is well. As soon as this substance dwindles, through age or infirmity on the part of the queen, the hive will begin to take steps to replace or super-sede her by raising new queen cells. A queen may continue to rule for a number of years without interruption and lay many thousands of eggs. Eventually the sperm from the mating, which is stored within her body, will become exhausted and her reign will come to an end.

The worker

By far the greatest proportion of bees in the colony will be workers, up to 100,000 in a hive although it is more usual to see 50,000 to 80,000. These workers are unmated females and only in rare circumstance will they become able to lay eggs (if they do so, these eggs will only hatch into males). At first glance the workers appear to be the same as the queen but with practice you will observe the queen to be slightly larger. The workers, as the name infers, carry out all the many duties in a hive. It has long been thought that there is a natural and automatic progression in the duties carried out by the worker. After growing from an egg into a fully developed bee within its sealed cell in twenty-one days, the worker emerges and immediately begins to carry out its predestined role. Within the first few days of life she will be employed cleaning out vacated cells for the queen to refill with eggs, or cells for storing pollen and nectar from returning field workers. She will remove any waste from the hive, perhaps stand guard at the entrance to deter unwanted visitors, or simply fan with her wings with many others to circulate the air and control the temperature within the hive. The worker bee will meet foragers returning with nectar and take the proffered nectar from their honey stomachs into hers and transport it to be stored and converted into honey. If required she may be fed by the others and induced to produce wax in tiny sheets from special glands on the last four visible segments on the ventral side of her abdomen.

After some weeks on cleaning duties she will exit the hive on fine days and take short flights to familiarize herself with her surroundings and take important bearings from the sun to permit her to find her way home. Then, when required, she will begin to forage, flying up to three miles or more each time to gather nectar, pollen, water or 'propolis' to bring back to serve the hive.

The worker will continue to fly and forage for about six weeks, when she will become literally worn out – the 'fur' on her body will be worn away, her wings may be tattered and torn and she will rest for the last time, often far from home.

Having said all of this, some exciting recent research has shown that the hive may be able, by using extra heat on the developing larvae, to predetermine the role of the foraging worker. The extra heat is provided by so called 'heater bees', which can raise their body temperature by vibrating their wing muscles. This has been observed in research hives by the use of a camera showing the

Bees at hive entrance. (Courtesy The Food and Environment Research Agency, Crown Copyright.)

Propolis

Propolis is the 'mortar' that cements the hive, fills in cracks and crannies and, along with wax, forms part of the cap used to seal cells containing larvae, pollen or honey. It is normally gum that exudes from pine trees and other plant sources but has even been found to contain molten tar from the roads! If a large invader enters the hive, such as a mouse, and is successfully killed by the hive, being too large for them to remove, the corpse will be completely embalmed with propolis.

---

temperature in different colours. If this is true it adds a fascinating dimension to the currently held belief of a 'hive mind', or intelligence within the colony, and may indicate that all is not predetermined by genes.

The term 'busy as a bee' is one with which we are all familiar; it infers that all these creatures are working hard all the time. Research has shown this to be far from true. In periods when there is no nectar to fly to or when the weather is inclement, the hive will often contain up to a third of the population surplus to requirement, resting, waiting for work and probably getting in everyone else's way!

The drone

Anyone reading about the drone could form the opinion that this bee has the best job in the hive, but read on. Drones are produced later in the year for only one purpose: to mate with a queen if required. And while he is waiting for this opportunity he does no work, he is permitted to help himself to any food and (rather strangely), should he choose to fly abroad, he will be permitted entry to any hive he wishes.

He looks a little different from the queen or worker – slightly more 'chunky' in appearance, somewhat darker in colour and with rather large eyes. Apart from being male, the only other essential difference we need to consider is that he has no sting – and this is his Achilles' heel. In the autumn, when his services are no longer required and food is getting short, he will be unceremoniously forced out of the hive, or even stung to death. Life is even shorter for the males that are fortunate enough to fly and mate with a queen. In the act of mating, their genitalia and parts of their intestines are torn from their body and they fall to earth to die!

ANATOMY OF THE BEE

I did promise this book would not go into great detail on such matters (there are far more detailed descriptions in other books), but we should know what the bee is made of, so to speak. It is an insect capable of flight over many, many miles. Its single pair of wings is normally folded back along the body when at rest. Like all insects it has no supporting internal skeleton but is encased in a rigid shell, or exoskeleton, protecting its soft inner parts.

The body consists of a head with a very efficient pair of compound eyes (eyes that have many lenses) like the common housefly and many other insects. The head is equipped with a normal jaw but no teeth. The jaw is used for moulding and shaping wax and propolis, but the bee cannot ingest solids; instead it has a modified tongue that forms a tube through which it sucks up nutrients, nectar and honey. The tongue is automatically extended when sense organs at the front of the mouth detect nectar or similar fluids.

Next we have the thorax, a sort of chest containing the heart and other organs but no lungs. The bee does not breathe through its mouth but obtains oxygen through a number of small vents like portholes along each side of the exoskeleton. It does not have red blood but rather a clear liquid, correctly named 'haemolymph', which serves to move the oxygen around in much the same way as blood does in animals (for the purposes of this book we will refer to it as 'blood').

The bee has a bulbous abdomen with a very thin waist. The abdomen has a normal stomach as well as a special 'honey stomach', which is capable of holding quite large amounts of nectar compared to the size of the bee and which most importantly contains an enzyme that helps to turn the nectar into honey. When the bee has visited enough flowers to fill this stomach, and it may be many hundreds of flowers, it will return to the hive where it will regurgitate the nectar into the mouth parts of other bees on hive duty; they in turn will pass it from bee to bee via their honey stomachs and eventually deposit it into a prepared cell in the honeycomb. Here the excess water in the nectar will be evaporated off, the enzymes from the honey stomachs will have done their magic, and we have honey.

Finally, at the bottom of the abdomen are the anal gland, the reproductive organs and the sting. The sting of the worker bee is barbed and connected to a small muscular sac containing the venom and it is this venom that causes the pain we feel when we are stung. Unfortunately for us, and for the bee, when she stings us the barb will not withdraw, as our skin is too tough. The sting, with sac attached, is torn from the bee's body and she will die through loss of bodily fluid. The sac, however, will continue to pulse and inject venom into us or any creature unfortunate enough to be so inflicted. When smaller enemies receive a large number of stings it may eventually cause death. It would take many hundreds of stings to kill a healthy human in normal circumstances. Above the sting is the Nazenov gland, capable of exuding a scent which is used by the bee to call other bees; often you will see a stationary bee at the hive entrance fanning its wings to disperse the scent and attract other bees.

The body of a bee is covered with small hairs, almost like fur; these are what make the bee so invaluable to the flowers they visit. In search of nectar, the bee brushes amongst the reproductive parts of the flower. This will ensure that pollen grains from the flower's reproductive system stick to this fur. In moving from flower to flower the pollen is brushed onto parts of other flowers and the flower is thus pollinated, meaning it can produce seed or fruit. Now the hard-working bee has to stop from time to time and using its legs, which have a sort of comb on the inside, it combs the pollen from its fur and thus down into a collection of longer hairs on its back pair of legs called the 'pollen basket'.

The Nazenov gland

The Nazenov gland, named after the scientist who identified it, has an interesting function. It gives off a scent that can be identified by the human nose, but most importantly it serves to guide the bees. When the bee stings, some of this scent is sprayed onto the skin of the victim, telling other bees where to go and sting. If you are stung, remove the sting and quickly blow some smoke from your smoker over the area to disguise this scent.

Corbicular pollen loads. Note the brilliant colours. (Courtesy The Food and Environment Research Agency, Crown Copyright.)

It will continue to pack these full until they contain a small pellet on each of the back legs. The correct term for this pellet is the 'corbicular load'. It is easily visible to the naked eye and may be an eighth of an inch long by about half as wide. Inspect such a pellet and you will see that it has been packed hard and contains many thousands of pollen grains. The colours will vary from almost white to a deep, reddish brown, depending on the variety of flower it has been visiting.

The pollen provides the protein the bees require. In simple terms, honey is merely a rich carbohydrate fuel to power their body, in particular the powerful wing muscles; pollen is their source of protein, to build body parts and to make new bees.

BUILDING A BEE

Into a prepared cell the queen will deposit a fertile egg, one of 3,000 or more she may lay daily in the height of the season. To the naked eye these small eggs appear almost like the reflection of light shining on the small amount of liquid food deposited alongside them, and the sight should bring joy to the beekeeper – it means the hive is healthy and producing new workers. The bees maintain a constant temperature within the brood area and for three days after the eggs are laid, the nurse bees add a quantity of 'royal jelly' to each cell. Royal jelly is a very concentrated food and is only fed to the workers for the first few days. The larvae in queen cells are fed almost exclusively on it. From then on the workers are fed on 'brood food', the name given to a sort of pre-digested mixture of pollen and honey, containing all the nutrients the young grub needs. The grub is incapable of movement apart from the odd wriggle and cannot survive without food being brought to it. The grub just lies there in a bath of food and eats!

Cells on a honeycomb, showing eggs and young larvae in the bottom of the cells. (Courtesy The Food and Environment Research Agency, Crown Copyright.)

During the next five days the grubs are fed every few minutes and grow at an astonishing rate. Gradually the food is reduced to a more simple diet of honey, pollen and water. The grub changes its 'coat' five times as it rapidly grows out of the old one. After this period, the white curled up grub stops eating and straightens out in the cell, head pointing outwards. Now the attendant bees seal the cell with a ventilated cap or cover of wax, or wax and propolis, and the grub begins to change internally. It spins a silk cocoon and within this cocoon the organs form, the outer soft skin is replaced by the tough exoskeleton and the grub changes into a bee. Twenty-one days after the egg was laid, the young bee emerges and makes its way to the nearest supply of honey to feed. Within minutes it joins the throng of worker bees, cleaning, feeding, and fanning the air and so on as the hive dictates. Nurse bees move rapidly to the newly vacated cells, clean out all traces of the last occupant and prepare the cells for the next batch of eggs.

WINTER BEES

Having described how the bee in summer may live for only a few short weeks we must explain how the bee can survive for the many months of winter. During the autumn the hive raises a large number of bees that essentially contain a higher proportion of body fat. These workers are the same as the summer bees, and look no different, but since their role is to lie almost dormant in a cluster around the queen, they have no need for much flying or foraging, except perhaps for water and to defecate on fine days. They will move around and keep the hive clean, repair any cracks or leaks that occur and are always ready to repel invaders. Mostly they form a tight cluster in the centre of the hive, retaining the warmth and moving from outside to centre in a slow rotation to keep each other warm.

As spring approaches they will fly to find early nectar but by this time the hive has already begun to produce new bees to replace them. The queen will have begun to lay a few eggs as early as January, just a few a day at first then gradually increasing as the days lengthen and the warmth of the sun returns and the cycle continues.

THE BEE DANCE

This has been described many times and you will easily observe it in the hive when manipulating. The returning foraging bee will do a dance to alert and inform the other members of the hive as to the distance, direction and value of any nectar she has discovered. In simple terms, the vigour of the wriggle indicates the value of the find, the direction or line of the wriggle shows the direction of the discovery, and the size of the circle she makes after the wriggle line indicates the distance. Bees will gather around to obtain this information and to sample the smell of the nectar she has found. There is little doubt that this is an inherited characteristic but it is so fascinating to witness, the bee will not even pause in her dance when you lift out the frame she is on!

BUMBLE BEES, WASPS AND HORNETS

The bumble bee can be found in environments similar to the honey bee, pollinating the same crops and working just as hard; in fact, they begin working much earlier in the day and continue long after the honey bee has retired for the day. The difference is that this bee does not make honey. For them, life begins with an over-wintered, mated female finding a suitable nest site, usually an old mouse nest. It raises a few young, keeps a supply of nectar nearby, the colony raises new queens which go off to be mated, and these will then find somewhere to hibernate over winter. The old queen and all her workers die off in the autumn.

It is a similar story with wasps and hornets, although they feed their grubs with captured insects, which they kill and chew up to feed to their young (they themselves prefer to feed on nectar, jam or anything sweet!). Having raised a family throughout the summer they also die off in the cold autumn. Only the mated young queens survive to hibernate in cracks, crannies, lofts and garden sheds throughout the winter.

However, a final word in praise of wasps, not often heard from a beekeeper or anyone else for that matter: please do not be too swift to kill them or destroy their nests unless you have to. The wasp is a pollinator, although it is not as efficient as the bee and cannot give us any honey. During the period of writing this, I observed on my daily rounds that there were fewer bees about and many more wasps. When the so-called Boston ivy covering my house is in flower, there are normally thousands of honey bees pollinating the flowers; this year there were very few but they had been replaced by many hundreds of wasps.

There is a saying that nature abhors a vacuum, and this was a perfect example – in the absence of bees, the population of wasps had taken over their role to good effect. Remember also that as part of its lifestyle, the wasp captures many insects, chews them up and feeds them to the grubs, and as a reward receives a drop of honeydew (the sweet liquid excreted by aphids) on which she feeds, as she herself cannot eat solid matter. This is why wasps become more troublesome in the autumn. The colony has ceased raising young so the remaining adults cannot obtain food; they turn to ripened fruit, and any other source of sugar, especially your jam! They are simply starving to death. Most of the insects she kills are the 'pest' of gardens and their inhabitants, so, at least until the bees recover, spare that rolled-up newspaper!

It is high time man learned to respect nature and cease interfering; we can only wait for the natural order of things to be restored, and in the meantime, perhaps Nature knows best?

CHAPTER 2

HIVES AND EQUIPMENT

For the purposes of this chapter, the 'hive' we refer to is the home in which we keep our bees. It may be somewhat confusing that the home and its contents have the same name – sometimes the bees are referred to as the 'swarm' or 'colony' but most usually as the 'hive'.

THE HISTORY OF THE MODERN HIVE

Man has long kept bees for the valuable honey they provide; long before sugar was available it was his only source of sweetener for his food. There is evidence that bees were kept by the Egyptians along the Nile River as many as 6,000 years ago. The earliest manner of beekeeping was destructive. Often a hollowed-out log was used, and later the attractive woven straw skeps. A swarm of wild bees would be encouraged to set up home as early in the spring as possible and the owner would protect them from the weather and from predators until the autumn. The bees would then be killed and their honey taken – this did little for the welfare of the bee! It also

contributed to problems with swarming today, since all bees were essentially those that naturally swarmed and the inherited tendency is now difficult to eradicate.

The evidence is that, certainly in the UK, bees were a valuable asset. They were jealously guarded and cared for, and the remains of stone recesses in walls of outbuildings

White painted WBC hive. (Courtesy E.H. Thorne (Beehives) Limited.)

Wall constructed to contain 'skep' hives. (Courtesy J.C. Jeremy Hobson.)

show that shelters were built for their simple hives. Local laws dictated that if a swarm were being pursued in order to 'take it', as long as the pursuers beat on pans to alert others as they followed the swarm, they alone had the right to take the swarm. The explanation of the traditional rhyme, 'A swarm of bees in May is worth a load of hay, a swarm taken in June is worth a silver spoon, a swarm of bees in July is not worth a fly', is that the earlier a swarm can be secured and housed, the greater the possibility of them making much honey; a swarm late in the season has little value. The fact is, beekeepers had no option but to destroy the colony to harvest the honey and accepted it as readily as having to kill their animals to secure meat.

Fortunately for the bee, over 200 years ago some enlightened beekeepers began to study this creature in the hope of improving matters. They knew that in the wild, the bee survived in colonies over the winter, and that if they could keep them, there would be no need to take a chance with a wild swarm in the spring. They discovered that bees were quite happy to inhabit any shape of space and could easily adapt to a square box.

Study a colony of bees, in any shaped void or box, and you will observe that the core of the colony inhabits a round shape covering many frames, rather similar in size and shape to a football (and hopefully, larger!). The odd corners they will fill with stores of pollen and honey close at hand for the growing brood.

Brood frame in the process of inspection. (Courtesy E.H. Thorne (Beehives) Limited.)

Diagram of section through hive, showing the frame located on runners and illustrating the bee space.

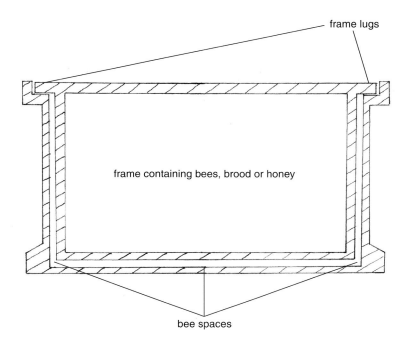

frame lugs

frame containing bees, brood or honey

bee spaces

This core is where they concentrate the eggs and growing brood in order to control the temperature, and in the winter the colony retreats into this area to keep warm.

Now, if this box could be fitted with removable frames, the honey could be taken without too much harm to the bee. And to achieve this, by far the most important discovery was that of the 'bee space'.

The bee space

The bee space is the optimum space a colony will allow between frames or combs and is left for the purposes of access; it is approximately ¼ inch in size. Spaces smaller than this will be filled up with propolis or wax. Spaces greater than this will be filled with brace comb, which is odd sections of honeycomb.

Armed with this discovery the modern hive as we know it began to develop. As with all developments, it soon became clear that boxes of different dimensions were fine but did not permit interchangeability. This was found to be a problem, since with standard sizes one could swap boxes between hives to increase yield, or between beekeepers to pass on new stocks. Eventually a number of standard sizes became in common use and the system we use to this day was born. Why then, you may ask, are there so many different sizes of hive on the market? Why not just have one size for the whole planet? The answer is quite simple: a colony is more efficient and (more importantly) happy if it has space to grow. If they do not have room it may well encourage them to swarm to find more suitable quarters. We can help them by adding more boxes; however, in some parts of the world this would lead to an unmanageable stack of boxes at risk from the elements.

Strangely, one of the largest types of hive, the Modified Dadant, is very popular in the former Russian states. Whilst their winters may be harsher and longer than ours, when the spring returns the development of the colony is rapid and the bees need to be able to expand accordingly.

PARTS OF A HIVE

In basic terms, the hive consists of a floor, then a number of bottomless four-sided boxes, each with a ledge at opposite sides to support the ends of a number of frames. These frames hang parallel to each other with the bee space between them.

Foundation is the name given to beeswax sheets, of sizes cut exactly to the frame designated. Wired foundation has a reinforcing wire embedded in it to make it stronger and less likely to bow or collapse under the weight of honey or brood. The shape of the base of the cells is moulded into the sheet and the bee will then draw out this shape to construct the cells. Foundation ensures the cells are

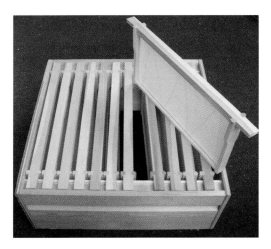

Brood box and self-spacing frames fitted with wired foundation. (Courtesy E.H. Thorne (Beehives) Limited.)

uniform and assists the bee in providing some of the wax she needs for the task.

One can purchase all frames ready assembled and fitted with foundation or, more usually, the frames come as a set of parts and the foundation is bought separately. In any event you will soon have to learn how to replace foundation, so the latter option, apart from its cost saving, will teach you much. The frames may be glued or not according to taste, and then pinned together with special thin pins – a steady hand and a small hammer are called for! One can purchase a tool called a pin push, which, as the name suggests, is a tool that holds the pin or small nail in a tube and by exerting pressure on the handle the pin is pushed into place. Once again these frames must be assembled perfectly square but fitting foundation at the same time will almost certainly ensure you have: if you have to force in the foundation, or worse, try to cut some off, you have done something very wrong!

The frames will be filled by the bees with honeycomb. The first box is called a deep box or brood box because it will contain the brood. Some hives may be fitted with a second deep box if the hive is vigorous and the honey plentiful. On top of this will usually be a crown board, something like the ceiling in a room, followed by a weatherproof lid or roof. When the honey flow starts, the crown board will be replaced by a 'queen excluder' and then a number of shallow boxes or 'supers' designed to store the surplus honey.

Many beekeepers use the deep box for the purposes of storing honey above the queen excluder, and if the honey flow is good and your bees vigorous, it may well be a good idea. However, some people find them very heavy to handle if filled to capacity and the shallow super more manageable. The bees show no preference.

TOP LEFT: *Hive inspection, full brood box. Note the wired queen excluder on the ground (right front). (Courtesy Rupert Stephenson.)*

TOP RIGHT: *Crown board showing mesh fitted over feeder holes.*

RIGHT: *Inside a hive, showing the queen excluder in position. (Courtesy Rupert Stephenson.)*

The purpose of the queen excluder is just that: the queen when in egg production is a little fatter than the worker bee, and the excluder, made either from sheet zinc or plastic with slots punched in it, or preferably made of stainless steel wires across a wooden frame, acts rather like a sieve. This is placed on top of the brood box, a shallow or super box is added, and the workers can now go up and draw out honeycomb but they can only fill it with honey as the queen cannot get through to lay eggs. This makes removing the honey far more kind to the bee – one does not have to kill any young brood amongst it. At the top of the hive is the all-important roof. Usually clad in zinc or aluminium, this roof can be flat or a pent shape; the bees really do not seem to care as long as the wet is kept out. Deeper sided roofs are available for windy locations to prevent the roof lifting off in a gale.

The usual material for construction of hives is timber, mainly cedar; this can be painted or treated with a non-insecticidal preservative to improve its weather resistance. Timber has the advantage of being cheap and durable, it

Home-made hive stand with alighting board attached.

Hive stand with standard floor in place.

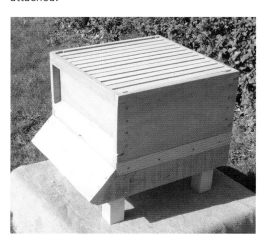

Hive with brood box and frames assembled.

Crown board fitted in position.

Dummy super or eke fitted to permit the use of a feeder.

offers good protection and a degree of insulation and it can be simply manufactured with only basic tools.

There a number of different types of hives in use today, in this country and throughout the world. All these different hives may have different dimensions and therefore parts will not be interchangeable, making life very difficult on occasions when you may need to shuffle things around, as you will read.

The most important decision you will need to make is which type you will adopt of the hives described. Your local beekeeping association will help you and it is wise to use the

Hive complete with deep roof covered with roofing felt.

BELOW: Large apiary in a garden setting. Note the collection of different hives – this hobby just grows! (Courtesy E.H. Thorne (Beehives) Limited.)

same type as most other beekeepers in your area. Swapping hive parts and other equipment is essential unless you have very deep pockets, even then you will miss the most important part of beekeeping.

Having said that, beware – beekeeping can be addictive and the hobby grows: over time one hive can become many and you will almost certainly 'inherit' bees and equipment from the partners of beekeepers who have gone to the Big Hive in the sky. As a result you may end up with a motley collection of types of hive, always intending to re-house them in one type but never quite achieving it!

With some care and skill you may be able to make your own hives; however, for the sake of the bee, they must be robust, accurate, and free from any bad joints, as there is little room for error. It may be difficult to obtain the correct sized timber required: even with modern adhesives and biscuit jointers, unnecessary joints are to be avoided. However, many manufacturers in this country produce the finished article; cut by machine they are very precise and one can even obtain them as a flat pack for home assembly, complete with all fixtures and fittings. The pack will include full instructions for assembly and even the glue is supplied. For many this is by far the preferred option and one can be sure of a satisfactory product. Later perhaps, you may wish to make some simple parts such as floors, stands or a pretty roof.

Demonstration at an agricultural show. Note the green plastic spacers on the frame lugs. (Courtesy Rupert Stephenson.)

FRAMES

We speak much of the frames, so it is well worth looking at them in greater detail. Essentially they are four pieces of accurately machined timber, usually pine or cedar. The top may be wide or narrow – wide tops help keep the bees down whilst working, a matter of taste. Most tops have a ¼-inch lug at each end to ensure the accurate bee space although plain topped frames may be fitted with plastic or metal clips that have the same function. Be careful in attempting to mix the two or you will end up with a double bee space between frames. They will not all fit in the box and the bees will soon fill up the gaps with brace comb making manipulation very messy. Under the top of the frame is a narrow slot designed to accommodate the foundation. The sides of the frame may either be two separate thin pieces of wood which fit either side of the foundation or a solid piece with a groove to accept the foundation. If the latter, then the bottom consists of two thin pieces; if the former, a single piece.

The other way of using foundation is by the use of 'ekes', often used in either deep or shallow supers intended for honey, particularly where cut comb is called for. A narrow strip of unwired wax foundation is cut from a sheet and fitted into the groove under the frame top. With care it can be secured with a hot iron or even a heated nail held in pliers (you don't need a lot of heat, just enough to melt the wax and 'stick' it in place). This then will give the bees a start and they not only draw out the foundation strip but will continue to fill up the remainder of the frame, and the comb can be cut from the frame when full of ripened honey. The object may be economy – a single sheet of foundation can be used to fill five or six frames by this method – but I have yet to work out what the saving is if the bees are having to manufacture their own foundation instead of making honey (it has been said that it takes the bees five pounds of honey to make one pound of wax).

TYPES OF HIVE

The first hives we will examine are all single-wall hives, that is they are simply a box, or boxes, made of one thickness of timber, and all share the simplicity required for ease of manipulation. We begin with the smallest.

The Smith

Named after the designer, it has the same internal capacity as the larger National, but is made more compact by virtue of having short lugs on the frames enabling the box to be made smaller. It is a very popular hive for those who wish to move hives in order to pollinate crops and very common in areas where the hives are moved many miles to the heather crop when it is flowering. Smith hives

also have locating pegs in the base of each box to prevent them sliding about during transport. This hive is very popular in the North of England and Scotland. If you are able to secure some Smith hives at reasonable cost, by all means go ahead, as they are a good hive, but remember you will not be able to interchange parts with the National (although National frames can be adapted by cutting off part of the top frame or lug). A member of a beekeeping society I once belonged to stated that the National was invented for people who are afraid of bees because the short lug of the Smith means one's fingers have to be much closer to the bees to remove the frames! This may be so, but I find the longer lugs easier to manipulate and I can think of no worse situation than dropping a full frame of bees! The Smith is a top bee space design but this is built into the hive box, not the frame, so although the frames may be interchangeable with some cutting of the lugs, the boxes, which are smaller, are not.

The National

Correctly, the British National, was so named as it was the first attempt to introduce one common size for the British beekeeper. This is a very popular hive that has much to commend it. In the variable British climate it is large enough to accommodate a decent sized swarm and in very good seasons can be simply extended to allow for a larger colony. The parts are easily obtainable from the many stockists and many of your beekeeping friends may already use it. As always, check with your local beekeeping society. The frame size is 14 inches by 8½ inches, it has long lugs and is a 'bottom bee space' design (as this implies, the bee space is at the bottom). Very much recommended for the beekeeper with limited space and budget who is content with a modest honey crop, the National can, however, produce very good results. For those demanding a larger brood box, the National can now be purchased with a deeper brood box and frames to increase the capacity. However, it becomes messy to change things over once occupied by bees and one should plan to start with this deeper box if possible.

The Langstroth

Once again named after its designer, a very famous beekeeper, The Langstroth is very popular in certain parts of the world, particularly the USA where its larger size allows for a greater area of comb and can accommodate a larger colony without the need for adding a double deep or brood box. A growing number of beekeepers here and on the continent use this hive but none of the parts are interchangeable with the National or Smith and the initial cost is higher. Before considering this hive it is, once again, wise to check locally: if, as most beekeepers do, you wish to share honey extractors, the frame size may be too large to fit them. The frame size is 17⅝ by 9⅛ inches.

The Dadant

This is the largest hive we shall consider; in much use on the continent, the frame size of this beast is 17⅝ by 11¼ inches. If could be suitable if you have a colony vigorous enough to fill it and the honey flow sufficient to fill the boxes, but just consider the weight of the boxes! They are available in the UK and are starting to become popular. Those with large and vigorous colonies find them easier to manipulate than a double brood box on a National, and the brood box has almost double the capacity of that hive. Only once

did I ever have any experience of them and the weight of the boxes; when full it is quite alarming to someone used to the National. Having said that, if I were starting again, I would most likely chose the Dadant. A friend in France has 1,000 Dadant hives in use and it is noticeable that each brood box has been constructed with stout folding metal handles for ease of lifting.

All the aforementioned hives are single-walled hives. We now consider the only double-wall hive of note.

The WBC

Named after the inventor William Broughton Carr, this is a very attractive-looking hive with its pent roof and pretty stand. The design is meant to keep the bees warmer in winter and cooler in summer and has much to commend it. However, it is more difficult to manage, more expensive to buy and maintain, and even though I have had only a brief experience of it, I could not get on with it. Basically it is a double-walled hive, the inner box having an outer box, or 'lift' surrounding it, and this in my opinion becomes fiddly. (I do not wish to argue with anyone who uses them; if you like the ideas, and bear in mind the interchangeability problem, by all means go ahead.) For my part, on the aesthetic viewpoint, I have built National hives with a pretty pent roof and an equally attractive stand to the satisfaction of the beekeeper who likes the look of them, and for me, this gives the best of both worlds. There is a story regularly told at beekeeping meetings, credited to so many people that it is now almost apocryphal. The story is that a member was praising the pent roof over the flat roof because it sheds rain better; another member replied that he had never seen rain piled up on a flat roof! I doubt the bees really care.

On the subject of looks, this is very much a personal matter. The purists amongst us like to keep things simple: pent roofs take up more space, as do alighting boards – if you are moving hives around they will always get in the way. Stands look very nice but the bees will notice no difference if their boxes are simply placed on a couple of bricks, or cement blocks, or even the ubiquitous plastic milk crate.

However, if you have only one or two hives and you wish them to be a feature in your well-kept garden then go ahead. If you construct the alighting board as part of the stand then the basic hive can still be removed if required and the pretty pent roof can be replaced by a simple temporary flat roof if the need for moving arises. The important thing is for you to enjoy keeping the bees, and taking pride in the appearance of their home is not harmful.

HIVE MAINTENANCE

The cost of a hive is not cheap; once you have made this investment it is wise to protect it, by protecting the hive from its worst enemy, the weather! Wood kept dry and free from insect attack will last indefinitely but its second worst enemy is paint. Moisture gets behind the layer of paint and begins to rot the wood (observe bubbles and cracks in wood that has been painted). There are now on the market some wonderful microporous wood stains in many hues and colours, which permit the wood to breathe and, more importantly, keep out the wet. Another type of preservative is the spirit-based and water-based wood treatments but check carefully that they do not contain an insecticide or you will kill your bees. Creosote used to be very popular but is not now freely available. If you have some, it can be used on floors but they

must be fully dried and vented in the fresh air for a week or so as the fumes are rather toxic, and it is best avoided.

Finally, none of the inner parts of the hive should be treated – the bees will do a very good job of that!

Before parting with hard-earned cash, you should join your local beekeeping society – something I advocate in all cases and make no apologies for repeating. Here you can discover which hive is in common use in the area; after all, you may wish to swap bits and pieces from time to time. In the main, beekeepers are lovely people and their help is worth gold. Having the same equipment will be a distinct advantage: this author did once painfully have to cut off the lugs of three National frames which were full of bees and grubs to donate them to a friend who had lost all his bees but who failed to tell me in advance that he had Smith hives. Neither the bees nor the author were amused, but we all survived to tell the tale. The greatest truth ever told is that people rarely learn from the experience of others, only from their own. If all you lose is some money, that's hard luck; if you lose or kill a bee through ignorance or neglect, then that is shameful.

GENERAL EQUIPMENT

Browse through the catalogue of some of the manufacturers and suppliers of equipment and you may be put off beekeeping for life! In these catalogues are many items that years ago were devised and made by beekeepers, for example, the stand with alighting board attached and the solar wax extractor, which are now made by suppliers in response to demand, but a little skill and determination can save you a lot of money.

The list seems endless, but the amount required to make a start will be more

*Through-section diagram of a
simple solar wax extractor.*

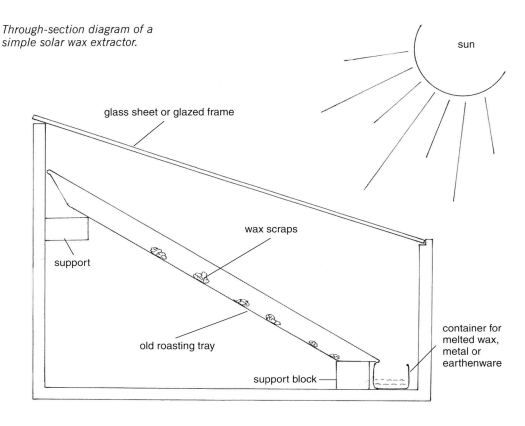

manageable and much equipment can be borrowed from other beekeepers. However, there are some items that you must obtain for yourself, as you will certainly need them frequently during the summer months and your friends will need theirs!

Most certainly you will need your own smoker (a tin, copper or stainless steel container with a simple pair of bellows attached). Fuel in the form of hessian sacking, corrugated cardboard or the new timber-based pellets are ignited inside the smoker and the lid with its nozzle is fitted, so that by pumping the bellows from time to time you get a supply of smoke. The aim is to keep it burning gently without undue heat. If you can run it to it, the latest idea is the clockwork

smoker which has a small motor driven by a clock spring; this powers a small fan inside giving a supply of air and keeping the fuel alight.

The next item you will require is a hive tool. In an emergency you can adapt an old chisel but the standard hive tool has a hook for levering up the frames at one end and a scraper at the other for removing brace comb or excess propolis in order to re-fit the frames. There are more elaborate and expensive hive tools available but it may be better to start with a simple and cheap option.

Last but by no means least you will need a bee suit, which is very much a case of personal taste and the size of one's pocket. They range from a quite simple and inexpen-

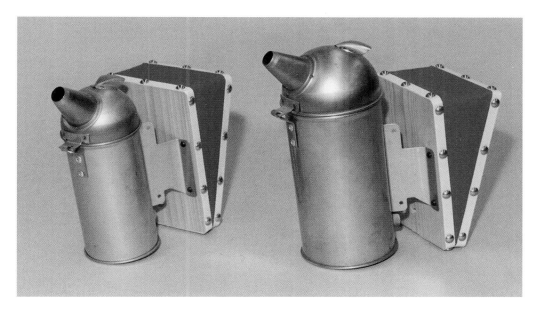

ABOVE: *Two sizes of copper smoker. (Courtesy E.H.Thorne (Beehives) Limited.)*

BELOW: *Clockwork smoker. (Courtesy E.H.Thorne (Beehives) Limited.)*

sive hat with a veil attached. These are an ideal first purchase anyway as if you later progress to a full suit it will be useful to protect visitors. The next stage of protection is offered by the jacket and veil. This is a white cotton or similar material jacket with elasticated waist and fitted with a veil. The arms and upper body now all receive protection and many beekeepers are content to use them. At the top of the scale comes the full bee suit, rather like a set of coveralls with a semi-rigid helmet equipped with bee proof visor. The full suit offers the beekeeper great confidence and should offer full protection. However, I would add that in hot weather, if wearing little under-neath, the bee can sting right through (as I know to my cost) – it is very unlikely but it can happen. To my mind the perfect suit is the one manufactured from what appears to be a silk-like synthetic material and it works beautifully for one reason: in order for the bee to drive home her sting she must grip with her feet, but the shiny material does not afford her any purchase. I have seen bees on such a suit

attempt to sting and the effort simply lifts their feet off the material. A further advantage is that they are not as hot in warmer weather as the traditional materials.

When purchasing a suit, bear in mind that you may have to wear extra clothing under it on cooler days and allow for the space, since a loose-fitting suit is more effective than a tight one.

Gloves are a matter of taste: some people find they make manipulation difficult and clumsy; others find them essential. The pair shown above is made of thin leather and has attached cotton sleeves which are elasticated and prevent stray bees running into them. There are thicker gloves available which are guaranteed sting-proof, but many find them clumsy in use.

ABOVE: Gauntlets (centre) with standard hive tool, a jar of French acacia honey (left), and a block of reclaimed beeswax (right).

BELOW: Deluxe hive tool. (Courtesy E.H.Thorne (Beehives) Limited.)

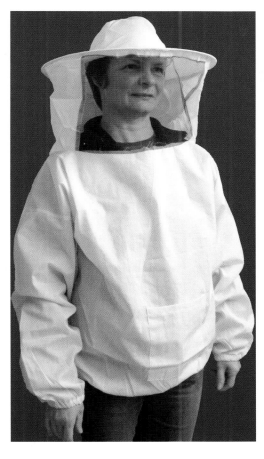

LEFT: *Bee jacket and veil. (Courtesy E.H.Thorne (Beehives) Limited.)*

RIGHT: *Full bee suit. (Courtesy E.H.Thorne (Beehives) Limited.)*

CHAPTER 3
SITING THE HIVE

As important as choosing the right hive in the first place is placing the hive in a permanent location before you house your first bees. Having chosen your location with care, ensure you do not later wish to move it as this causes difficulties. There is a rule commonly agreed on concerning moving bee hives: 'less than three feet or more than three miles'. Research has shown that bees mainly navigate by the sun; even on a slightly overcast day they can use the sun to orientate themselves and find their way over many miles. When they get close to their 'target' – be that either their home or a source of nectar – they then use recognizable landmarks to guide them. If you move the hive just half a mile away, for example, the bees will exit as normal and do not detect a great enough difference in their location to make any changes and merely fly to the nectar, but on returning are guided to the previous location of the hive and they are lost. Move them more than three miles and as soon as they exit the hive they realize they are located differently in relation to the sun's rays. They will re-orientate themselves according to their new location before flying off and will return successfully.

Near to the hive, the bee will have used various local markers to find her hive, for example a tree or fence post, even a shed or another hive, and she uses this to make her 'final approach' to the hive. If this hive is moved less than three feet at a time over many weeks she will adjust her information and find the correct hive. More than this and she will have great difficulty finding the hive and she and her sisters may be lost.

Accordingly, it seems most sensible to locate the hives where you intend them to remain, for at least a full season. There are a number of considerations to examine, not least the needs of the bees themselves and the good temper of your neighbours! The wise man will take the trouble before starting this project to visit his immediate neighbours, to explain what he intends to do and seek their approval (the promise of a jar of honey at the end of the season will do much to secure their consent). Better this than begin a war of attrition which could result in you having to locate your bees elsewhere.

If possible, the entrance to the hive should face south or close to it, as the warmth will help the bees get up to work early. The hive should be sheltered a little from the prevailing wind, ideally behind a hedge rather than a solid wall or fence. A hedge permits the wind to 'bleed' through it, slowing the wind and dispersing it; a solid wall will cause downdraughts as the wind goes over it and down the other side. Commonly used in urban gardens is the 'ranch-style' fence with alter-

Aerial view diagram of suggested hive base.

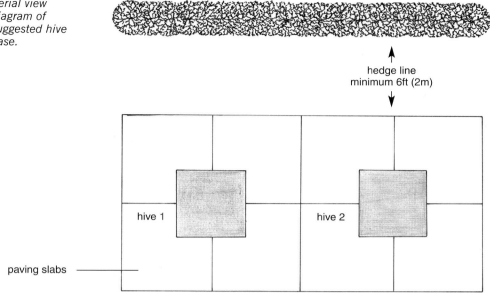

hedge line
minimum 6ft (2m)

hive 1

hive 2

paving slabs

nating boards each side of a central post. These are ideal as they permit the wind to bleed through in the way suggested.

The hive should be at least 6 feet (2 metres) away from any fence or hedge to permit access to the hive and to ensure the bees have room to go up and over easily when they forage in that direction. Beware of siting a hive below overhanging trees – there may be too much shade, too much moisture dripping from the trees, and in the autumn the area will be a mess of leaves. An open aspect is much to be preferred if possible.

Ensure that the plot you have chosen remains firm all year. Whilst it may be so in the summer months, low-lying places may become waterlogged in winter to the detriment of your hives and yourself when visiting, and, as it is low lying, it may also be a frost pocket (that is, cold air will run down hill and if it cannot flow to lower ground, it will form a pocket of frost surrounding your hive), which will not be enjoyed by the bees.

Next, consider the flight lines the bees will take. If they are near, for example, a footpath, or a neighbour's garden, there may be complaints and it is wise to avoid them. Consider also your own, or your neighbours', washing line: bees have a need to defecate, especially on a fine day following bad weather when they have been forced indoors. The very fine day when the washing is on the line, your partner or neighbour may take exception to the white washing being covered with yellow spots!

A final consideration is dogs: bees do not share your love of them, so ensure they are kept at a safe distance. If you have a dog, however kind its nature may be, you must consider fencing the area securely from dogs, as the dogs' natural curiosity may not be appreciated.

Many illustrations depict a hive placed on four bricks on a lawn, very picturesque but totally impractical – what happens when the grass grows? Even raising the hive on a stand, there will be problems in cutting the grass close to the hive and underneath it. Bees do not like lawnmowers or strimmers and unless you choose to visit after dark with hand shears, they will not appreciate your presence much either. Better by far to plan the whole thing with care and be able to ignore it for the season. Cement paving slabs are an excellent solution.

Better still, lay a sheet of landscape fabric or other permeable membrane down first, to deter weeds from growing up through the gaps between the slabs and permit any surface water to drain through. Then lay a number of slabs in a square or rectangular area at least 3 feet (1 metre) larger than the hive, to allow you to stand during manipulation. Consider also making the new base larger, big enough to accommodate a second hive. You may not initially intend more than one but this hobby can be addictive and two are as simple as one to manage.

If properly constructed, this area can enhance the garden and such a construction will not need much attention for many years. Importantly it will make your visits much more enjoyable; to be standing on firm level ground while you work is a definite asset. During a period of his illness I once visited a friend's site to manipulate the bees for him. They were not the friendliest of creatures but I had become used to them. The site was rough grass in an orchard, and of course I tripped and fell – not the best situation, but no permanent harm was done and the scars soon healed!

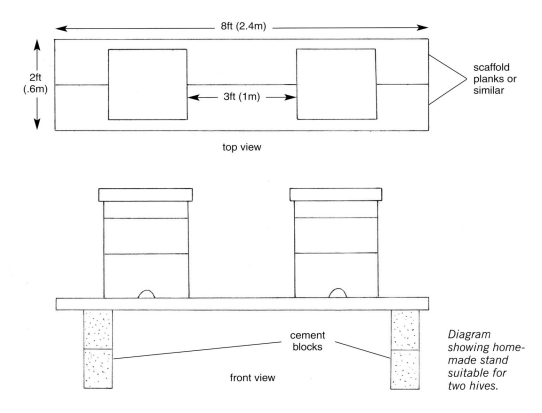

Diagram showing home-made stand suitable for two hives.

Having now produced a suitable place for our new friends and before their arrival, assemble the hive on its stand to make sure everything is ready, and put in a hive block to prevent a feral swarm from occupying your one and only hive.

At this stage you must make another decision that may affect the bees and cannot (or should not) be altered once you have chosen: whether you wish to align the frames front to back, or side to side. Front to back is called the 'cold way' because the air entering goes straight up into all the frames. Side to side is called the 'warm way' because the first frame tends to block the incoming air. It is currently thought that in summer, and particularly during the honey flow, the cold way enables better ventilation and permits the bees to climb the frames more speedily, whereas the warm way is better in the winter; but you should not change them around at will. If your hive site is sheltered, the cold way may be best; if exposed to cold winds all winter, you may consider the warm way. I have heard equally convincing arguments for both but must leave you to decide, most hives of my experience have been aligned the cold way.

An active hive will require a large quantity of clean water and the thoughtful beekeeper should provide a constant supply. If you have a birdbath in your garden, this is ideal, as the shallow water at the side permits the bees to take a drink without fear of drowning. A simple bowl will suffice, placed high – on top of a wall or flat shed roof could be ideal. Place a large stone or half brick in the middle and the bees will alight on this island before going down to the water's edge to drink. Keep the water clean and fresh. To be even more confident of a clean hive, the water bowl should have a low roof to keep out airborne disease. I am not sure this is essential – after all, you cannot deter a neighbour's bees from

Front of hive showing frames aligned the cold way, front to back.

Front of hive showing frames aligned the warm way, side to side.

visiting, nor can you ensure your bees drink only at your local, but I mention it in passing. What is important is that the water is clean, fresh and plentiful.

One final thought on site preparation: place a house brick or similar on the ground a metre or so from your hive. When manipulating the hive you require somewhere level to stand your smoker, as the base is very hot and will burn grass, or worse, fall over. Many beekeepers, including this one, have tales to tell of damaging equipment by leaving a hot smoker standing on it.

INSTALLING YOUR BEES

At last the day (preferably a fine one) dawns when your bees are due to arrive. It is likely that your bees will come in what is called a 'nuc' or nucleus box, which is a box containing four to six frames with a healthy small colony, or nucleus, complete with a young mated queen. If this is the case, prepare your chosen site by moving your hive back a little to permit the box to stand in the spot where your hive will live. It is also a good idea to have a small potted shrub, if you have one, to stand in front of the entrance; if not, a bucket filled with sand or soil with a piece of branch stuck in will serve. Stand this about 1 metre away from the entrance of the nuc box. As soon as the bees arrive, or you have collected them from the breeder, the sounds from within will tell if all is well – if all is silent, anticipate disaster. Assuming all is well, take the box to your stand and place it in position. By all means remove any seals on the box but do not open it just yet, as the bees will be very unhappy and may come out all in a rush and be lost. Time for a cup of tea!

Put on your bee suit and light your smoker (you will not need much but it is good practice). When you return to the hive site, all should have settled down and the soon-to-be familiar sound of gentle humming should be heard. The shrub or mock plant in front serves an important purpose: when you open the entrance, the bees should not fly straight out, and they will see the shrub and exit in a more orderly fashion using the shrub as their first locating beacon to find their way home. Give them a little smoke, stand to one side and open the entrance, then move a little distance away and observe. You should quickly notice that the bees who have flown out are dancing up and down just a few feet in front of the box. They are orientating themselves with the sun and landmarks, and preparing to go to work, initially for water, perhaps to defecate and later to begin the cycle of nectar and pollen gathering. If the day is dull and overcast, or raining, fewer bees will exit but the action will be similar as described.

Now is the time to withdraw and let them get on with things. Resist the urge to bring friends and neighbours around to view, and leave them in peace. As the sun begins to set, quietly return and observe from a distance – the bees should be returning and going to bed for the night, they will come to no harm in their temporary home.

The next fine day, or as fine as one can expect, the bees should be ready for placing in the new hive. If the weather has turned inclement, they will come to no harm for a day or two; if it is fine and sunny, they can be housed the next day. Around noon, suitably attired and armed with your lit smoker, perhaps assisted by an experienced keeper, open up your new hive and remove all the frames from the brood box. Give the nuc box a little smoke and wait a moment or two. Gently remove the lid, use your hive tool and remove the first frame. Place it in the centre of you brood box and place a new frame of foundation on the outside of it, then repeat the action until all the frames from the nuc box are in place and in the same order as they were received. Add a new frame to the far side of the pack then gently manoeuvre the whole lot until they occupy the centre of the brood box. This is not the best time to examine each frame but a quick glance should tell you all is well. If the queen is marked, as she should be, you may even spot her on the frame, which is a good sign. Fill the remaining spaces each side with new frames, remove the nuc box and return the hive to its rightful place, ensuring you have removed the hive block! Put on the crown board and the roof before examining the now vacated nuc box. There may be a number of dead bees in it and probably also some live ones wandering aimlessly about. Stand the box against the front of your hive and they will eventually find their way in. *Do not shake the upturned nuc box over the installed colony.* The last thing you wish to begin with is debris and dead bees in your clean hive: if the bees are fit, they will find their way in; if dying or injured, they are best left outside.

Stand back and observe – the bees should now enter and return as if they had always lived here. Enjoy the moment. For now, for better or for worse, you are a beekeeper.

Over the next few days, progressively move your shrub back from the entrance, a foot or so at a time. The bees will quickly adapt and eventually it can be removed altogether.

It may be part of the terms of sale of your nucleus that the box they travelled in is returned to the vendor, or if they have been supplied by another local beekeeper, he will certainly wish to have the box returned. If this is the case, clean the box thoroughly before returning it. Make no attempt to sterilize it, the owners will certainly do this, but give it a good clean and return it promptly. Alterna-

tively, the box may have been included in the price of the bees; some suppliers insist you collect your bees by appointment and they will inform you if the box is included in the cost. The box may well be very cheaply made of thin plywood and will not take any serious use (it was not designed to), but it will serve again and, most importantly, in the winter months you can use it as a pattern to construct a more solid version for your own use.

One minor drawback to being a beekeeper is that you may frequently be called upon by the local constabulary to deal with swarms. It is illegal to destroy them and even if the bees are not required at home you are almost duty bound to try and remove them. A well built nuc box equipped with a few clean second-hand frames of comb is the best thing to encourage a new swarm if either they have not settled too long or not invaded someone's loft, but that is another story.

MOVING HOME

The fact of modern life is that we are becoming migratory in our habits, for employment reasons, to enlarge our personal brood chamber or conversely for downsizing, but if you wish to take your colonies with you it should not present too great a problem.

If the new home is less than three miles from the old, you will have to consider boarding them out with a colleague for a few weeks (remember the site must be at least three miles from both the old and the new site). This may be a good option in any case, since your bees will be out of harm's way while you make the move and you will have time to construct a new site.

Assuming the new site is far enough away, you will then have to consider two possibilities: either that the new occupant of your old home

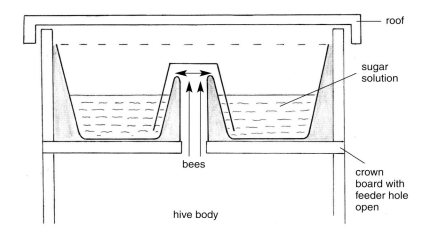

roof

sugar solution

bees

crown board with feeder hole open

hive body

Section diagram of a feeder.

gives you permission to leave the hive or hives where they are for a few days while you construct the new site; or that the vendor of your new property will permit you access to do so at your new home before you move in. They will in all likelihood correctly insist that this is arranged through the respective solicitors.

When you come to move the hive, some extra preparation is needed. Unless you are using a Smith hive which has locating lugs to keep the boxes from moving, you will need to temporarily fix them together. There are special brackets available for the purpose but I have successfully used the flat triangular brackets from Meccano sets. Screw everything together and finally put a strap, or straps, right over the top and down under the floor. If it is at that time of year, first clear down and remove any honey supers and move them separately; if not the burden will be unmanageable, and the supers can be replaced later.

Once again, when installing the hive on the new site, use the 'bush in the pot' system, permit the bees to settle and release them as soon as they have done so. This way all should be well and within forty-eight hours they should continue to forage as before.

Check after a few days that there is nectar coming in. There may well be less in the area initially and it may be prudent to add a feeder of 'one-to-one syrup' to help them while they discover new sources. One-to-one syrup is one part sugar to one part water, which will serve as a temporary stop gap when bees are short and as an emergency feed when required, but is not strong enough to deter the bees from gathering the nectar they prefer. Always ensure you remove the emergency feeder when it is no longer required as it can attract moulds.

A final word on neighbours: they may consider, for example, a large and noisy dog to be an acceptable pet for a neighbour to have, but some have strange misconceptions about bees. The best way forward is to beg or borrow a spare bee suit or two and invite them to see your bees – once they witness these charming creatures you may have another convert to the beekeeping fraternity. Take time to explain the lifestyle of your bees, especially the possibility of them swarming; better that than the embarrassment some of us have endured of finding half your colony in a neighbour's tree just as they were planning a barbecue!

CHAPTER 4

HANDLING YOUR BEES

Many years ago there was a method of beekeeping – namely, 'Leave them alone' – which today would invite disaster, but we do sometimes need to handle our bees. The reasons are fourfold.

- ▣ Firstly, we need to ensure that our bees are productive, that there are sufficient food stores to raise the brood, that the queen is laying fertile eggs and that the workers are able to manage all the queen is laying.
- ▣ We need to assess when and if we should add honey supers. To add them very early in the season can be a strain on the resources of the hive. Warming the space above them to permit the brood to hatch, by progressively increasing the space in the hive, makes the hive more productive.
- ▣ If that is our chosen method of controlling the swarming instinct, we need to open the hive at intervals of no more than fourteen days and 'pinch' out any queen cells before they develop fully and the hive prepares to swarm.
- ▣ Most importantly we need to monitor any disease or pests that may be present. As in all things of this nature, prompt action early on can avoid a disaster and ultimately save your bees.

There are a number of factors to consider before you begin to handle your bees, not least of which is yourself. Bees are not naturally aggressive but on occasions they may be defensive – there is a difference. Like it or not, they identify you as an intruder and under certain conditions may act in a defensive manner, their only defence being to sting.

Certain scents can irritate the bees, and their sense of smell is very acute. Firstly, never go to your bees after a hard day's work without a shower, and do not apply strong deodorants. Likewise they do not like the smell of animals, in particular dogs; again, ensure your clothing is fresh and clean. The scents of leather belts or watch straps also annoy them.

One course of action I would thoroughly recommend is to befriend someone at your local beekeeper's society and arrange to go with him and work his bees. Most beekeepers are pleased to be asked. If he or she was taught as I was, you will first watch as a hive is worked. Stand close, keep quiet and pay attention, for the next action should be the beekeeper inviting you to work his next hive, under supervision. And if he was as good as my tutor, the next act should be for you to work the next hive and 'teach' the owner! This is a wonderful way to begin for it makes you recall all you have been told and in explaining it to someone, it is forever imprinted on your mind.

Wear a good, well-fitting bee suit or hat and veil, and good-quality gloves if you wish (many find they make manipulation difficult, yet others have no problem). Lastly consider the feet – or more accurately the ankles and trouser bottoms. In defence bees will normally attack the head and upper body; however, should a bee or two land on the ground near your feet during operations, they may find a way up the inside of your clothing. Eventually they may find things tight and restrictive, or you may try to dislodge them, and the result can be painful. Disrobing to discover the culprit whilst handling the bees with an open hive may not be the best option. The most secure method is to wear wellingtons and tuck one's trousers or bee suit firmly inside. A good friend preferred to use bicycle clips.

PREPARATION

Now this is all common sense but needs to be considered, in particular if you are working alone. Ensure you have all you are likely to need during the operation and put it close to hand. Your smoker, hive tools and perhaps a bee brush may be obvious; not quite so obvious may be a frame or two of clean foundation, an empty brood box or 'dummy', a clean replacement floor and manipulation cloths. If you have a friend helping you, make sure before you begin that he or she is aware where your spare parts are and can get at them. The aim is to have the hive open for the least possible time, as even the most obliging bees can get annoyed with you.

MANIPULATING THE FRAMES

Choose a warm sunny day if possible, at about midday, when at least some of the bees should be out working and will not trouble you. Beware if there is a thunderstorm imminent, as bees can sense the drop in barometric pressure that accompanies a storm and become defensive.

The first thing to do is make sure your smoker is working well – if you are new to the

Inspection with assistant. Note the box of new frames ready at the rear of the hives. (Courtesy E.H.Thorne (Beehives) Limited.)

The dummy box

The dummy deep or brood box is very useful: if you have spare brood boxes, then there is no need, but if you have not, and have some basic carpentry skills, you can fabricate a simple box of the approximate dimensions. This can be used to stand any frames in that you remove as you work. Many beekeepers merely prop the frames against something but I know of more than one who inadvertently stepped on it later. The dummy box keeps it upright and out of harm's way. Just remember, never use the dummy in your hive, as the bees may not appreciate your workmanship!

---

hobby, an hour spent practising with this will pay dividends. Properly filled and lit, all it should take is a few pumps every now and then to keep a satisfactory supply of cool smoke available (only experience will tell how often is 'now and then' and whilst working bees is not the best time to practise).

We begin with a few puffs of smoke into the entrance, which will cause alarm in the hive. The bees, fearing fire, will rush to fill their tummies with honey ready for flight. Give them a few minutes – remember, they have to travel to the nearest honey and take a drink – then remove the roof, lift the crown board and give a few puffs of smoke in the gap. Once more, give them a few minutes to react. Lift off the crown board and place it safely nearby. Describing your actions from now on is not easy – better that you watch an experienced beekeeper first – but I would best describe it as smooth and purposeful. Move your hand, for example, close to and very quickly over the frames and you will almost certainly receive a sting or two; move your hand in the manner suggested and the bees will ignore you.

If you intend to use manipulating cloths, this is the time, before the bees well up out of curiosity. Place the rolled up cloth, one part on each side and in line with the frame's direction, then unroll the one side to cover all but the first frame. Whether you work right to left or vice versa is a matter of choice and, of course, if you have chosen to align your bees the warm way, for 'left to right' read 'front to back'. Perhaps add another puff of smoke over this exposed frame but never overdo it, as too much can antagonize the bees. With the hook end of your hive tool, gently break the bond under each end of the frame in turn (the first frame will be the most difficult as all are packed tight and stuck together), then gently pull out the first frame and examine it. The frame will probably contain very little, since the brood will usually be in the middle frames and unless space is restricted, the

---

Manipulating cloths

Manipulating cloths, like most equipment, can be purchased but many beekeepers (or their long suffering partners) make their own. They consist of two separate units of a square of heavy cotton cloth, even old curtain material (colour is not an issue). The square should be a little larger than your hive to permit a slight overlap, and should be affixed to a length of square timber about 1 inch in diameter and a little longer than the width of your hive. The cloth can be fixed to these wooden strips with staples, or woodworking glue.

frame may only have been partially drawn out or contain just a little honey or pollen on the inside. However, if it is full of capped honey, when you have completed your inspection, put on a queen excluder and a 'super' of honey frames. Remove the frame and store it as suggested, away from any clumsy feet.

Roll back the cloth to uncover the next frame, and unroll the other side to cover the space. Break the bond on the frame lug, lift out and examine, then put the frame back in under the cloth at the side of the box. If you observe odd lumps of brace comb, gently scrape them off with the chisel end of the

Examining the frames

When examining frames, one should avoid turning the frame on its horizontal axis. The comb has been constructed to take the load in a downward direction, so turning the frame in such a way will expose the comb to a load which could bow the contents, or worse, cause the comb to fall.

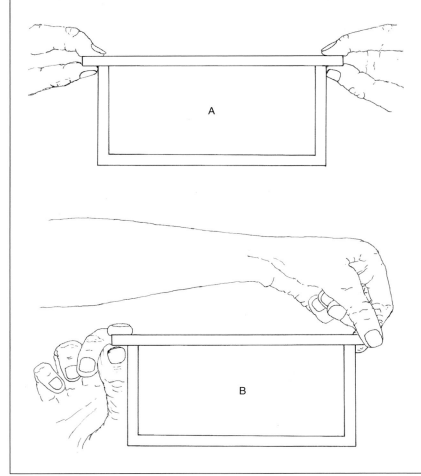

The suggested method of turning frames during inspection.

hive tool, as they may get in the way when you reassemble. Many beekeepers save these oddments and melt them down (*see* page 82). You then progressively work through the frames in the fashion described until all have been dealt with.

What are you looking for? For many, it is the queen cells, slightly larger than normal and protruding from the frame, tucked into odd corners, and there may be as many as a dozen or more of these. It is a sign that the hive is preparing to swarm and action should be taken now. As we will discuss later (*see* page 56), a common way to deal with this is to pinch out and destroy these cells; repeated

Marked queens

Marked queens are queens that have been identified by a blob of paint on their back, just below their head, the colour of the paint indicating the year in which she was raised. The internationally used colours are white for years ending in 1 or 6, yellow for years ending 2 or 7, red for years ending 3 or 8, green for years ending 4 or 9, and blue for years ending 5 or 0. The marking for the year 2011 is therefore white.

Inspecting a brood frame showing brood in the centre of the frame, and sealed honey stores in the upper corners.

every two weeks or so, this will delay or frustrate the swarming but it is not the only answer. However, if you see them you have little option but to do this or suffer a swarm in a few days, by then it is too late.

You are also looking to see if all appears healthy. If you are fortunate enough to spot the elusive queen, all is well (if she has been marked it will be somewhat easier). If there are many cells containing eggs or grubs then this is a good sign that all is well and you can close up the hive as soon as you have finished. The queen is often difficult to spot, as she will scuttle to the far side of the frame and back again when you turn it, often protected by the workers. With practice you will find her, most often in the centre of the brood box, but to generalize would be incorrect.

The corners of the frames will usually contain stored honey and pollen. This is the bees' ready-use larder and if it is well stocked, the hive is healthy. Compare the stores each time you go through the hive and you will soon learn if these stores are depleted and the hive could be short of food. There may well be long periods where, although there appear to be plenty of flowers in the area, the weather is not suitable for the flowers to produce nectar. It is at this stage that you may need to consider summer feeding.

Assuming all is well, the whole set of frames remaining can be pushed back into their previous position and the spare frame that was removed first should be carefully replaced.

As your hive and the frames become older and soiled, it is a good idea to leave out the first frame removed. Take a look at the frame, and if there appears to be no brood or stored honey but the bees have begun to draw out the foundation, then keep it out. When you complete your inspection, instead of pushing the frames back to their original position, put a new frame with foundation into the last space. Remember to do this the same way each time and eventually you will be able to replace all your frames with new ones. The bees will always centralize their brood area and the much-used central combs will eventually work their way to the outside and be relegated by the bees to a minor storage role or disregarded altogether.

At this stage, while all is open and moveable, it is not a bad idea to replace the floor if you have remembered to bring along a spare. The floor gets covered in debris, even in the best of hives, and a sterile new floor will do much to prevent disease. The old one can be removed to your work area and sterilized and prepared for exchange next time.

Double brood boxes

Working a double brood box is exactly the same, except that the top box is first removed and placed nearby. I find a piece of white cotton sheet placed on the ground keeps everything tidy, and once the box is replaced, any stray nurse bees can be shaken into the hive or the alighting board. Cover the box with either the crown board or a spare cloth. Provided you are not too long in dealing with the first box, all will be well; a little smoke now and then will concentrate their minds. After completing the work on the bottom box, you replace the top brood box and continue as before.

I tend to assess a beekeeper by the number of squashed bees I see between the boxes – with just a little care, you should kill very few. As you place the boxes back together, they should first be carefully aligned at an angle to each other, taking care to brush aside any bees on the top. Then, by slowly realigning the boxes, any bee wandering about on the top of the lower box, or the bottom of

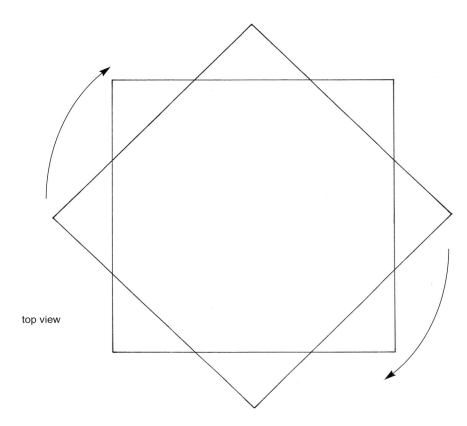

top view

Diagram illustrating suggested method of aligning boxes after inspection.

the upper box, will be brushed off, either inside or outside the hive, and very few bees need die.

AFTER INSPECTION

It is estimated that a hive takes about twenty-four hours to recover from your visitations. They have to reseal and repair any damage, and remove any cells you may have destroyed and any dead bees accidentally killed. It follows therefore that in this period they will make little honey and one should therefore avoid any unnecessary inspections.

Any frames that you have replaced should be taken back to your work area; those only slightly used are very valuable, and can be the basis of a nuc box or utilized in emergencies when taking a swarm, as the bees are attracted to the drawn comb. Place the frames in a sealed plastic bag and put them in your deep freeze for forty-eight hours or more (very few pests can survive this), and then store them in a cool shed, still in the sealed bag to deter wax moth. Never keep any that are badly soiled or damaged, however. Remove the comb, since the wax can be melted down and used as described later (*see* page 80). If the frames are sound they should be sterilized and repaired where

---

The honeycomb

Why is the honeycomb shaped like it is? The answer is as simple as it is clever: as the worker bee makes a cell, she stands on the base and builds the wall of wax around her own body, turning all the time inside it. The fact that the circular cells are placed close together in alternate rows means that the walls of the cells are in a hexagonal shape. The wood pulp cells of wasps and hornets display the same shape, designed to be economical in space (*see* illustration on page 15).

---

necessary before being fitted with new foundation and stored away from wax moths and other pests.

PUTTING ON SUPERS

As the season progresses you will notice during your inspections that the hive is starting to fill up, the middle is full of sealed brood or eggs and all appears healthy. Almost all the frames of foundation have been drawn out, even the outer side of the outside frames. This is a sure sign that it is time to put on a super for the honey. To delay now may trigger the swarming instinct, and in fact many beekeepers put the supers on much earlier than this and it is not a bad practice: when the honey flow starts, things inside the hive will change dramatically. Before you close the hive, first put on the queen excluder (*see* page 21) and then a super (either shallow or brood box size), fitted with frames of foundation. Then replace the crown board and finally the roof. In future inspections, this honey super should be put to one side and

covered while you inspect; a clean cloth underneath and a crown board or second cloth on top will keep all calm while you inspect the brood chamber.

TAKING OFF THE SUPERS

As the honey flow and the season come to an end, we must now consider taking off the supers. Filled or not, we must remove them, asses any honey we can take and return the remainder to the bees for the winter. There are on the market a number of types of 'clearer boards', all of which are designed to allow the bees back down into the main brood chamber and leave the honey free of bees; some do this more rapidly than others. There are also chemically treated quilts and sprays which force the bees down. However, the most simple and inexpensive method is to fit a pair of plastic Porter bee escapes into a crown board – the oval-shaped holes are designed to fit them tightly. If you have only one crown board, you will have to remove it with the bees in residence to fit these although it can be done while it is still on the hive. Better to remove it, and if necessary, cover the tops of the supers with a square of cloth. It is now that the value of a good friend with the same type of hive as your own becomes apparent, for this operation invites the defensive nature of the bee – they know what you are doing! The temporary loan of a crown board will make life much easier.

Assuming you have a spare crown board, remove the mesh covers from the holes and put in the Porter bee escapes. You will notice the bee escape contains a pair of sprung metal strips so that the bees can force their way through but cannot return. Apply some smoke as normal and wait. Remove the roof, then lift up the super and apply a little more smoke. Wait a few minutes, remove the super(s), then the queen excluder, and put the clearer board in its place. Replace the super(s) above the clearer board, replace the crown board and the roof, and retire. When you return twenty-four hours later, all the bees formerly in the honey super(s) will have gone down into the brood box and you can remove the supers without any aggression from them. The clearer board can be left in place until you return the emptied super(s) for cleaning.

STINGS AND WHAT TO DO ABOUT THEM

Before you consider keeping bees, consult your doctor. For most people the sting is just a nuisance and over time your body will become almost immune to them. Most beekeepers accept them as an inevitability and ignore them. However, there are two situations which could occur, one very serious and one less so, but for me to ignore them would be irresponsible.

The first is that you may have an allergic reaction to bee stings, or indeed any insect bite or sting. Usually this means the area around the attack swells up and over time can spread to, say, the whole hand or much of the arm and can be very unpleasant – though not life-threatening. The area may also itch and take days to return to normal. This is a histamine reaction and your doctor will in all probability suggest you carry a number of anti-histamine tablets to help with the reaction.

The second more serious condition is very rare and caused by a hypersensitivity to venom. If stung the victim can go into anaphylactic shock – a restriction of the muscles surrounding the bronchial tubes – and death can result unless immediate medical attention is given. The problem is that in some cases the victim is at a distance from medical attention. There are a number of beekeepers throughout the world who are prone to this condition; for them the answer is to carry an injection of so-called anti-venom, essentially cortisone, which will save them. It also follows that they should never work alone as they may be unable to inject themselves. I repeat, it is rare, but if you think you may be prone by all means consult your doctor and obtain the required medication. Giving up beekeeping is not considered an option by many people affected; in any case an accidental wasp sting will have the same result.

A CAUTIONARY TALE

This personal tale has been included to highlight some factors in handling, in mistakes that can be made, and as a thank you for the people who helped me. Some years ago I was gifted a swarm by a local beekeeper, who told me that they had been taken a few days earlier, they were in a box of the same type as my hive, and that he would drop them off. I prepared a hive stand and new brood body and awaited his visit. He turned up late, in a bad mood, and was in a hurry (not the best way to begin). He insisted that he would place his box on top of mine, that they would go down into mine and all would be well. His last words as he hurried off were, 'Let me have my box and frames back next week.'

Firstly, bees will rarely go down; they usually go upwards and it should have been a simple matter to reverse them once the friend had hurried away. When I took a look, however, the bees must have been in the box for longer than a week, and the reason he did not wish me to put my box on his was that the bees had drawn out wild comb from the underside of his crown board and it could not be removed! There were just four frames in the box, the frames were very old and decrepit and contained old and brittle foundation in them that had broken and had been rejected by the bees. For this reason the bees had drawn out wild comb from underneath the crown board, comb that could not be moved (which is why we use moveable frames in the first place).

I left them for one day to settle but decided that to delay longer would only make things worse. Before returning the next lunch time I tried to phone fellow beekeepers I knew to help me but all were at work or away from the phone.

I went to the hive and lifted off the crown board, hoping the combs would remain; my plan was to remove some frames from my brood box to allow space for the wild comb and I hoped the bees would eventually take over the frames of foundation either side of their wild comb. However, this wild comb filled the whole box, and was much larger than it would have been inside a moveable frame. The comb collapsed in a mass of very upset bees. Within minutes it seemed the whole swarm was in flight; at my feet were a mass of broken comb, broken frames, exposed larvae – the lot – and it would have taken a magician to repair and reassemble that mess.

I took a few steps back and took the proverbial deep breath, collected a piece of board to act as a ramp to the hive, removed all the debris so that I should not damage it further and pondered the situation.

As the dark swarm circled above me, I arranged the entire mass of damaged comb around the bottom of my ramp; this would attract some bees to recover the honey and pollen. They could not rescue the brood, which I knew was lost, and the brood would be what encouraged the swarm back. However, after retreating for a while to a neighbour's house for tea and sympathy I returned and noticed that the swarm, though mainly in flight, were now starting to settle. I stood for many hours watching the swarm surrounding me gradually settle onto the improvised ramp, then slowly the bees began to walk up into the hive and with joy I saw the queen in the middle of the first wave.

The mass of bees moved right into the hive, and gradually more flying bees joined them and followed them in. With my hands I scooped up as many nurse bees as I could and deposited them on the ramp. Eventually, just before dark, they had all gone into the hive, and I put on a summer feeder of weak syrup, arranged the mass of comb upright to permit them access and retired.

The next morning many bees were robbing the honey from the broken frames, but fortunately the bees were from the damaged hive, as my others were miles away. By dark of that day all was as clean as could be and I deposited the debris in the compost bin.

Of course the hive took a long time to recover, but eventually they did, and I learned the value of good advice, the importance of knowing when you have been told something inherently incorrect, and I did not receive one sting, something which during the event I did not even have time to consider.

It was not the best way to learn, but it is important to remember never to act through fear or panic; take your time to think a situation through, use common sense and the bees will usually comply.

CHAPTER 5

BEE TYPES AND STRAINS

One of the aims of the beekeeper over many years has been to produce a bee that is productive, relatively resistant to disease, but importantly, easy to handle. The accidental release of Africanized bees into North America produced a nightmare for their beekeepers. The Africanized bee is very productive and vigorous but beekeepers have to wear heavy protection in order to handle them, as they can be very defensive and will sting in great numbers when handled. Thanks to careful breeding and selection we now have a type of bee that is much easier to handle and they can be roughly grouped into separate strains for identification. Buying from a reputable source will ensure the nature of the product – before the disease Varroa wiped out many of the wild bee population it was very much a game of chance as to the nature of your captured swarm.

So-called 'strains' of bees are separated into different and distinct sub-species; add to this the natural hybridization of bees and you have an almost endless list of possibilities. Taking a swarm can be fraught with danger as, apart from the very real danger of importing disease, you will not be aware of the nature of your bees until they have re-established themselves, by which time any undesirable traits will have become evident and the only recourse may be to re-queen the hive. Better by far to choose a strain with the characteristics you require and keep them pure.

THE CARNIOLAN BEE *(APIS MELLIFERA CARNICA)*

Originating from an area of Europe ranging from Slovenia to the north Balkans, this is a very popular bee and with good reason. In appearance they are slightly slimmer than the English Black bee but they can be easily distinguished by their dull brown, greyish colouration and are sometimes called the grey bee. They are reputed to be able to defend themselves well against some insect pests but are known to be friendly and calm in handling. This strain has a better ability than some to respond quickly to rises in availability of nectar and to reduce in numbers when the honey flow ceases. When nectar is available it is extremely efficient in storing surplus honey and pollen. It also has a longer tongue than some strains, which enables it to take advantage of such crops as clover and alfalfa.

Because of their friendly nature they are very suitable for keeping in populated areas; they tend not to drift to other hives to rob honey. They will start work earlier in the morning and continue later in the evening

Moveable apiary of Carniolan bees in Slovenia. (Courtesy J.C. Jeremy Hobson.)

than some strains and they are particularly good at developing early in the season to take advantage of early spring flowers.

On the minus side, they have a greater tendency to swarm, particularly if over-crowded, and swift action should be taken to avoid this. Also the Carniolan is less tolerant of high summer temperatures, so shading the hive may be one answer.

THE ITALIAN BEE *(APIS MELLIFERA LIGUSTICA)*

This is another very popular bee and, as the name implies, it originates from Italy. It is a light-coloured bee ranging from a pale brown to an almost straw yellow, which is highly prized. The bee tends to build large stocks early in the year and maintain them through-out the season. They once had a reputation as being very defensive but recent stocks have been less inclined and they are now relatively easy to handle. They have always been prized for their ability to produce large stocks of honey and have less of a swarming tendency than some strains.

But this trait has its downside: they are notorious robbers from other hives and this contributes to them spreading disease from one hive to another. They have no better resistance to pests and diseases than other strains and this, along with their robbing tendencies, makes them less suitable for populated areas.

THE CAUCASIAN BEE *(APIS MELLIFERA CAUCASICA)*

Somewhat similar in colouration to the Carniolan, this sub-species originates from eastern Europe in the area of the Caspian Sea. They share many of the traits of the Carniolan, being easy to handle, and they also share the very long tongue that enables them to take advantage of flowers others just cannot reach. However, they do not have the Carniolan's ability to build up stocks rapidly in the spring and are therefore not good honey producers. They also have a very undesirable trait: they tend to use excessive amounts of propolis and are renowned as messy bees, making manipulation more difficult. Because of these factors they are not as popular as other bees.

THE BUCKFAST BEE

This is not strictly a sub-species, but a hybrid resulting in years of work by the esteemed beekeeper Brother Adam at Buckfast Abbey. Monasteries were always keepers of bees, as much for the honey to flavour their food as for the wax to make candles for religious purposes. In response to a near-disastrous outbreak of Acarine disease, Brother Adam set out on a long journey to produce a bee resistant to the disease. Based primarily on the Italian bee but somewhat darker in colour, he produced a strain that exhibited good housekeeping capabilities and reduced the incidence of infection. The bees also were able to tolerate the British climate yet produced good stocks of honey. Initially they were moderately defensive but later generations have become very difficult to handle and they can be the most fiercely defensive of all stocks. They are also slow to build up stocks in the spring so tend not to take advantage of the early nectar.

Brother Adam began his research into bees in the late 1920s and continued until his death over fifty years later.

THE RUSSIAN BEE

This bee originates from far-eastern Russia and has been introduced into the USA and the UK in an attempt to take advantage of its good resistance to Varroa. It is grey in colour like the Carniolan and Caucasian and, as its origin suggests, it is very good at tolerating hard winters. Moderately defensive and able to produce good honey crops, this bee is unusual in that it has queen cells present throughout the season and not just at times of swarming. Its main value appeared to be in its resistance to Varroa, having been exposed to it for longer than any other strain; however, in cross-breeding this resistant tendency diminished. Part of the enormous amount of research being carried out on a worldwide basis has been to attempt to fix the resistance to Varroa of the Russian bee into hybrids.

CHANGING THE STRAIN

Two sets of possibilities arise that would invite you to change the strain of the bees you keep. The first is that your bees have begun to exhibit undesirable traits such as a very defensive nature, or 'following' (here the bees will follow you in great numbers after you have visited them, and in a small garden this can be very troublesome).

The other possibility is that your bees appear to be not very productive even though fellow beekeepers report good results in the same season. Whatever the reason, all is not lost: the wonderful thing about bees is there is no need to dispose of the colony and procure another. By simply changing the queen, in the natural order of things the whole colony will change with her breeding; the older bees will have died out and you should get a brand new colony at the cost of the new queen, and in the meantime your bees will continue to forage as normal.

There are many established companies selling queen bees and they should be willing to forward details to you of the strain and nature of their product. To ensure purity of the breed, most of these queens will have been artificially inseminated. If not, no-one has control over the strain of the drones the queen will have mated with and it becomes a bit of a lottery with almost the same remote chance of a win.

When your new queen arrives, she will have instructions for her introduction and it would be confusing to repeat it here. In essence, one must remove the old queen first, then introduce the small cage containing the new queen and, in most cases, shut up the hive and leave it alone for a week.

It is important to stress that if your hive has become queen-less for some time, two things may have begun: either the hive may have raised a large number of queen cells, which if developed sufficiently may cause problems when you try to introduce the new queen; or the hive may have established a laying worker, which may well kill the new queen. It has been proven that the hive will often support the queen of their choice and assist in the demise of the less-favoured combatant. If one of the queen cells has hatched and a new queen emerges, the hive may take the side of their 'own' queen and destroy the 'alien' you are trying to introduce. Therefore it will be best to destroy or remove mature queen cells, and the hive will then more readily accept the new queen. I have not personally heard of anyone being successful in this, but, as in all things, I am ready to be corrected!

The act of introducing a new queen may appear a little daunting to the beginner and, as always, I advocate consulting your local beekeepers' society before taking any action. If nothing else you may save yourself some money by learning of a good source for your new purchase.

The result of changing a very defensive strain for one that is more manageable can be astounding. This beekeeper was filled with dread every time one particular colony had to be opened, and with good reason – the operation became like a major battle with casualties on both sides and the application of huge amounts of smoke to keep them down. Eventually the hive was re-queened. Two weeks later there was not much noticeable change, although perhaps I convinced myself there was; one month after that it was a pure pleasure to work them. I had inadvertently discarded my gloves and all I noticed was the inquisitive bees running over my hands as I worked – a real joy and what beekeeping should be about.

UNITING COLONIES

It frequently happens that a beekeeper has two, or more, very weak colonies for one reason or another – perhaps it has been a poor season due to bad weather, or a disease has decimated them but is now cured or under control. As the season ends you are left with the possibility of having to nurse them through the winter and perhaps lose them all. One option is to unite the colonies. First you must decide which colony has the better nature, or the qualities you wish to retain. By simply uniting the colony and letting nature take its course, you may well end up retaining the wrong queen. Better by far to select the one you wish to retain and dispose of the other. If you are forced to handle the 'good queen', remember to handle her with great care: despite the fact that she is capable of enormous efforts of egg production, she is very fragile, any damage caused to her may result in her being rejected by the new colony and you would then have a united but queenless colony.

Perhaps the simplest method to employ, having removed the unwanted queen, is to place the brood box of one hive on top of the brood box of the other with a sheet of newspaper between. Make a number of small holes, little more than pin pricks, in the newspaper first to enable one colony to smell the other. Then close up the hive. The bees will enlarge the holes but it will take them a little time, during which they will detect the smell of the new queen and their own, hive smells will mingle, and eventually (perhaps with a few minor skirmishes) the colonies will unite. Generally they will then be more interested in examining their new abode than fighting, after a few days the interior of the hive will be rearranged to their liking, and with luck they will prepare to settle for the winter as one colony. A beekeeping colleague has suggested that the process of uniting colonies presents a good opportunity to treat both units with the appropriate chemical to prevent Nosema (*see* page 85), as this also masks and mingles the scents of each colony.

CHAPTER 6

SWARM CONTROL

This is perhaps the most difficult aspect of beekeeping and cannot be learned in a hurry. There is no advantage in learning a dozen or more methods of swarm control if you have little understanding of the 'hive mind' and this is something which cannot be written; with some experience and good observation you will learn much and my best advice is to never be afraid to ask. Some beekeepers may well wish to keep their secrets to themselves, but most beekeepers will happily pass on much valuable information. It is in this way that a new pair of eyes, so to speak, may notice something that others have ignored as insignificant, and progress will be made.

Historically, beekeepers have been their own worst enemies as far as swarming is concerned and it will take many generations to rectify. As stated in Chapter 1, the original system was to capture a swarm of wild bees, keep them for the season and then destroy them to obtain the honey. It follows therefore that all bees were bred from those with a tendency to swarm, something we no longer want.

The bee swarms for one simple reason: to multiply and pass on its genetic strain. It is the only way it can do so and is a natural impulse. We are aware of the means by which it does so but no so aware of all the causes.

In preparing to swarm the hive raises special queen cells, much larger than normal cells and usually tucked away in odd corners; there may be as many as a dozen. The old queen has no choice but to lay her eggs in them but it is the way that the grubs are raised that makes them into potential queens. The young are fed an intensive diet of royal jelly, which is high in protein and turns the grub into the larger animal that becomes a queen; this is one of the many miracles of nature.

Eventually, as the new queens hatch, the old queen realizes her days are numbered. She summons her loyal followers – perhaps half the number of workers in the hive – and at a signal, the whole lot will stream out of the hive and gather in a cloud above it.

In that instant, the bees lose all memory of their previous home and will never return, and the swarm sends out scout bees to locate a new home. The body of the swarm, around the queen, will settle somewhere, perhaps on a branch, and may remain there for hours, perhaps days, until a suitable new home is located.

If you are quick enough, and have a prepared a nuc box, a brood box with frames, or indeed any suitable container, you may be able to take the swarm and start another colony, but if not they will be lost.

In the original hive, the new queen will fly

to be mated after a few days, and when she returns she may well destroy all the other queen cells to reduce competition. She will return from mating and very soon carry on as before, but with a much reduced retinue there will be little or no spare honey. In a worst-case scenario, further queens will hatch, the new queen will decamp with more bees, and so on until the hive is all swarmed out and barely viable. This is a disaster to be avoided at all costs. Worse still, the swarm that has left, if they find a wild location, will be prey to the diseases that have decimated the feral population in the first case and will be lost for ever.

However, the queen cells that exist in a hive which is preparing to naturally supersede the old queen may not have any tendency to swarm at all, so our interference at this stage may be a disaster. Some will tell you that in this case the number of queen cells will be fewer – sometimes only three or four – but how do we tell for certain?

You may be fortunate in having a hive which naturally supersedes itself: that is, when the hive discovers the queen is no longer as active as they require, they will produce a new queen. She may even live alongside the old queen for a while, then eventually the new queen takes over, the old queen is disposed of and all continues as before. For most of us, however, the reality is different and swarming is a constant battle. A hive that swarms too frequently may be remedied by replacing the queen with one from a strain that is reputedly less likely to do so, but there are many ways to reduce the risk of swarming and we will examine a few of them.

CAUSES OF SWARMING

Much has been written on the causes of swarming and if you have time and interest you can learn much from reading on the subject. What seems to be the most popular theory is a lack of space, or more exactly, the threat of it. The problem this appears to cause is an overpopulation of newly emerged brood. When there is a rapid increase in young brood and grubs ready to hatch, the hive senses this and begins to prepare to divide.

It follows therefore that to provide plenty of space may help to deter this mechanism. During your hive inspections observe if the bees have enough room to grow; if not, there is much you can do.

Firstly you can put on another brood box. Whilst most people manage very well with a single brood box on, say, a National and depend on the supers to give more space, it is undeniable that the larger the colony (provided it is healthy) the better the honey harvest, so a double brood box will give better results. At the end of the season it is a fairly simple procedure to reduce the colony back to a single box for the winter. There is now on the market a deeper brood box for the National which gives a lot more space. (I like this, as I always considered the shape of the brood frame to be too shallow: as stated earlier, the bee naturally makes a round ball-shaped colony.)

Putting on honey supers in good time will also help, as the honey is stored out of the brood box area and this leaves more space for raising brood.

It is also believed that an older queen may cause the hive to swarm and replacing her with a young, vigorous one will avoid the problem. The queen gives off a scent, called the 'queen substance'. When she is in full health and vigour, this scent will be passed from bee to bee throughout the colony and the bees know that 'all is well'. It is the presence of this substance that unites and controls the colony. As the queen becomes older and less vigorous, this scent diminishes

Bees clustered on the frame of a healthy hive. (Courtesy The Food and Environment Research Agency, Crown Copyright.)

in intensity, the hive notices and may begin to make preparations to replace her. Then, as the old queen becomes aware of the queen cells hatching, she may make arrangements to swarm.

Temperature may also play an important role and, as soon as practical, the hive entrances should be opened up fully to permit freer access and reduce the temperature. Carniolan bees in particular are known to dislike high temperatures, so give as much air as possible and even consider shading the hive in the hotter weather. Although all these factors may be contributory, none is a guarantee of success at deterring the swarming instinct, however.

What is certain is that one must treat each colony differently, as they may develop at different rates, and each season will be differ-

ent due to the weather and the availability of nectar. There is no calendar you can consult that will tell you when to commence each operation and only constant careful observation of the behaviour of each colony can instil in you an insight into the hive mind.

The most commonly used method of swarm control would more accurately be termed 'swarm frustration': every two weeks during the season, you go through the hive and pinch out any queen cells before they hatch. The hive then have to begin raising queen cells once more and by repeating the process, the season progresses without the swarm and your hive is intact. Many beekeepers consider this a necessary evil and dislike killing the queen cells, but there are alternatives – some simple, others complicated – that avoid this.

THE ARTIFICIAL SWARM

An 'artificial swarm' consists of the old queen with flying bees. This system requires quite a bit of extra equipment, but your local beekeepers' association may be able to help.

Assuming the colony to be divided has a brood box, queen excluder and two supers, you will also need:

■ a queen-marking cage (the cage enables one to isolate the queen and mark her with the colour of the year she was raised);
■ paint (Humbrol enamels will do the job) and a cotton bud;
■ a spare hive with floor;
■ a brood box with some drawn comb and foundation;
■ a crown board;
■ a dummy or empty super;
■ a syrup feeder;
■ quantity of two-to-one sugar solution;
■ a hive roof.

Before searching for the queen, remove the supers. Move the hive to be divided a short distance away and put the new hive on the stand where it was. The flying bees will return to the new hive, reducing the numbers in the original hive and making finding the queen less difficult.

If you can find the queen, put her on a frame, preferably of open brood, in the middle of the new hive on the original stand and the flying bees will return to her. The crown board must then be put on together with a feeder of two-to-one syrup. This syrup will enable the bees to produce wax and do the building required in the brood box. Keep supplying syrup while the bees keep drawing out foundation.

Because this colony has no sealed brood in it, Varroa treatment will be most effective, with oxalic acid using the trickle method (*see* page 87). This should remove most Varroa, giving the colony a good start.

The old hive with the brood and nurse bees under a queen excluder and with supers above it is located on its new site. The bees will not have been out of the hive so they will not return to the old site and the three-mile rule does not apply.

If you cannot find the queen, put the new hive with its empty frames on the stand on the old site. Take out three frames to make a space. Clear all the bees into it, making sure all the bees go in so the queen will be amongst them. Replace two of the frames and complete with a frame of uncapped brood from the original hive. This frame of uncapped brood will ensure the bees stay.

Put a queen excluder on the brood box with all the bees in it. Put the supers on this queen excluder, and the original brood box, which has no bees in it, on top of the supers. The nurse bees will move up through the queen excluder and the supers onto the brood in the top brood box, leaving the queen and flying bees in the bottom brood box. This is your artificial swarm.

After forty-eight hours move the top brood box and the supers to its new site and fit a queen excluder. This colony will be queen-less and will re-queen itself from the eggs or larvae in it, or you may have to provide a frame with eggs. Once the queen is established you will need to trap her and mark her with the colour of the year to distinguish her from the old queen should you re-unite the hives.

THE SNELGROVE METHOD

This is a system based on the use of the Snelgrove board, one of many systems devised by a truly great beekeeper, L.E. Snelgrove MA MSc, in his book *Swarming: Its Control and Prevention*. His systems proved what was previously thought to be impossible: to prevent swarming without the killing of queens or queen cells and without interruption of the honey gathering. In defence of commercial honey producers, I confess the system is not suitable for the large producer as it requires visiting each hive on important days and the owner of a large apiary just could not do it. For the hobby beekeeper, however, with perhaps one or two hives, it provides a fascinating insight into the hive mind and, above all, it is enjoyable and educational.

You will need:

■ A Snelgrove board (this can be obtained from your local equipment supplier, or you can make your own);

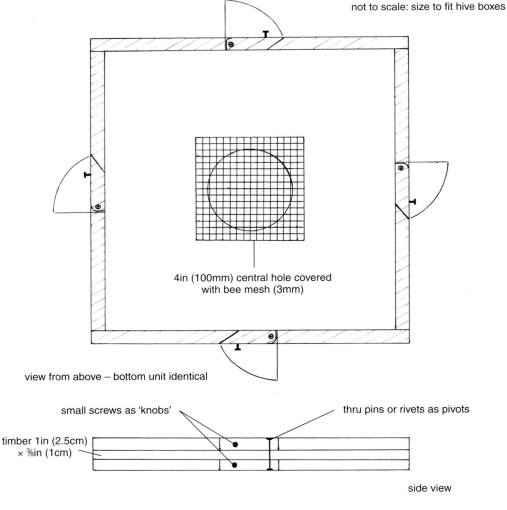

not to scale: size to fit hive boxes

4in (100mm) central hole covered with bee mesh (3mm)

view from above – bottom unit identical

small screws as 'knobs'

thru pins or rivets as pivots

timber 1in (2.5cm) × ⅜in (1cm)

side view

Diagram of a Snelgrove board.

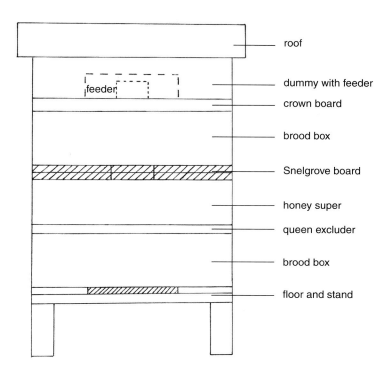

The position of a Snelgrove board in a single brood box hive.

feeder

- roof
- dummy with feeder
- crown board
- brood box
- Snelgrove board
- honey super
- queen excluder
- brood box
- floor and stand

- a brood box with frames of new foundation;
- a dummy super or empty super to accommodate the feeder;
- two-to-one sugar solution;
- a crown board;
- Porter bee escape.

Note that this requires less equipment than the previous system as the hive will be divided on the original floor, under the original roof and no additional stand is required unless you wish to divide the colony later. You may even wish to divide your colony at the end of the season and help another new member become a beekeeper as many of us do. For the beekeeper with limited space this system is ideal.

This system at first seems a little complex and I recommend that you read Snelgrove's book first in order to understand it. However, once you do understand it, the system is quite simple provided you can be in attendance at each important date. You only need to open the hive and manipulate the bees once; after that you are simply re-directing bees by opening and closing the small entrance and exit doors on the board at each stage.

Initially you open up the hive and separate the brood box into two parts: the lower part is to contain the queen, a frame or so of uncapped brood to keep her happy, and all the flying bees. The stage at which you do this depends on the season but it should be as the honey begins to flow and before the hive can make preparations for swarming. The bottom box is then filled with new frames of foundation and a honey super put on top of a queen excluder. Next you put on the Snelgrove board, which has a large central hole covered with bee mesh, and this permits the warmth from below to rise into the second brood box and also enables the two sections to be aware of each other. The second brood box contains all the remaining brood, sealed or otherwise, but must contain some newly laid eggs. A crown board comes next, followed by either an empty super or dummy to allow space for a feeder filled with two-to-one sugar solution. This is important as for the period of the exercise there will be little food brought in (as explained below).

The roof is replaced and one of the small doors on the uppermost side of the board is opened, allowing any flying bees in the top box to venture out in the normal way. The divided colony in the top box now realizes it is queen-less and begins to prepare a number of eggs to be raised as queens. The colony in the bottom box continues much as before: the queen is induced to continue to lay eggs by the presence of brood and the flying bees will continue to bring in nectar. Each seven days you open the door *under* the top door of the board, and close the top door above it. Then you open another top door on the opposite side of the board. The flying bees returning to the top box are now directed into the bottom box and will eventually find their way out through the normal hive entrance – they will continue to bring in nectar there and add to the stores in the original hive. Newly emerged flying bees from the top box (remember they are emerging and developing all the time from the brood we put there) will emerge from the new top door and fly to the honey. This is why we have had to add a feeder as they will bring in little food; as soon as they do they are directed down to the original colony. Seven days later the exercise is repeated, and the flying bees once more are redirected down into the bottom box. They are not rejected by the original colony as the hive scent, for want of a better term, is common to them all due to the contact through the central mesh. All this time the new queen is being raised and will eventually emerge to be mated. She will spend a few days as a virgin queen during which time she will in all probability destroy any other queen cells. After the third manipulation of the door, this new queen will fly to be mated and return to begin laying in the now much-depleted top colony.

After a further week open up the top colony, removing the feeder and dummy super. Look in the hive for the new queen and, more importantly, newly laid eggs – they can only have come from the new queen as all the previous eggs and brood will have emerged. If you find eggs, then all is well and the hive is ready, either to reunite or divide.

Once the new colony is established you have choices: you can leave all as it is and both colonies will continue to bring in nectar and make honey. The danger with this is that the bottom colony, which may now have grown considerably, may still try to swarm.

Another option is to remove the Snelgrove board and bottom super then re-unite the two colonies in the double brood box with the super (or supers) on top. This will give the new larger colony a lot more space and swarming will be avoided. Once again, nature

---

Help the queen home

Snelgrove suggests that at the time you anticipate the new queen will fly to be mated, you place a piece of brightly coloured card above the door she will exit to help her locate it as she returns from her mating flight. Failure to find the correct door may result in her entering into the bottom, original hive, with unwanted results.

Laying workers

It is possible that if no queen has emerged, the colony may have a laying worker – as she has not been mated she will produce only drones and the colony will eventually perish. If this happens you must seek her out and destroy her. Take a frame containing eggs from the bottom box and put it into the top box, then begin the process again.

---

will take its course: the queens will meet and the loser will be deposed leaving the stronger queen to carry on. It is noticeable that when this happens there is never any injury to the victor – the hive will decide the outcome and assist her.

A third option is to separate the two brood boxes into two separate colonies. One must be temporarily removed three miles or so for a number of weeks, or you can donate one colony to a friend; the original colony will now be too late in the season to consider swarm-

---

Queen balling

There is a process that has been observed both in supersedure and when uniting two colonies concerning the destruction of the queen, which is often called 'queen balling'. A number of worker bees will surround the queen to be disposed of, cover her completely and raise the temperature by vibrating their wing muscles. Eventually the queen dies either from the heat or a lack of oxygen (she is 'loved' to death).

---

ing and the new one will not be so inclined with a new queen.

To summarize Snelgrove's method, the hive has been prevented from swarming, honey has been brought in without interruption and you have had no part in the killing of queen cells every two weeks or so.

Snelgrove and others will offer you further ideas for swarm prevention and they should all be considered, for it is not an exact science. What is certain is that it takes a number of years to begin to understand the mechanism of swarming and perhaps as many again to learn how to prevent it. There is no shame in losing a swarm, for as I have said, you rarely learn from the experience of others, mainly from your own.

TAKING A SWARM

Once you have been registered with your local beekeepers' society, you may attract the notice of your local constabulary! When they receive information from a member of the public that they have a swarm of bees, they may call on your services. It is illegal to destroy bees, unlike wasps and hornets. In my early days, it was not just a challenge but often one could obtain a new stock of bees. Now, however, it is rather a two-edged sword: the swarm may have disease that can threaten your existing colonies and/or have traits that you do not wish introduce. However, we are duty-bound to attend and to try to rectify the situation. No book can ever prepare you for what you may find and I make no apologies for not listing each and every situation. What is certain is that bees will often swarm into the most inaccessible of places.

Firstly, be sure to go fully equipped with your suit and a smoker. Both may be needed: although swarming bees will rarely attack you, it does have the desired effect of keeping onlookers back! Take with you a substantial box or preferably a nuc with some frames of drawn comb, a sack or cloth to cover the box, your hive tool, a pair of good secateurs and a small pruning saw.

We will deal with the easiest (and rarest) situation first: the swarm has recently settled in a branch of a tree that can be reached from the ground, or from a low ladder. Suit up, take your small saw and slowly cut off the piece of branch they are on (beware – it will be heavy), carefully carry the branch with bees attached, open your nuc and rest the swarm on top. They will slowly go down into the box and after making sure almost all the bees have entered, close up the box and depart to rounds of applause! It only happened to me once.

More commonly, they will be settled on a branch that is too high or inaccessible to all but the longest ladder, the branch will be too large or difficult to cut, or may be well grown in amongst other trees and branches. I do not recommend the practice of standing on the top of a ladder with a box balanced on one's head waiting for the bees to go down, as it will seem to take ages. I did this once but would never do so again; I was later told it took over an hour, but it seemed like a week. The 'wait and see' system rarely works either; if the scouts have departed and discovered a suitable permanent location, it will in all probability be in someone's roof space and miles away.

And that is the next worse-case scenario: they have already occupied the roof space or, even worse, they have been there for a week or more before being reported.

A good friend devised a very ingenious piece of equipment comprising a vacuum cleaner, a large sealable box with some small mesh panels and a special reducing valve to reduce or increase the intensity of the suction. The theory was that by applying suction and using another length of hose attached to the box, he could gently 'suck' the bees out of such awkward places into the box, which was partly lined with foam rubber to cushion their fall. One has to reduce the suction from the vacuum cleaner or it would kill the bees. I believe it worked very well.

The alternative is a horror: working away in poor light in a hot and restrictive space, attempting perhaps to remove plaster board and insulation and eventually filling a box with wild comb, angry bees and all sorts. You pray you have the queen and most of her entourage before you eventually cover the box and make a retreat from a large number of very angry bees who will no doubt remain there for some hours.

But this is what beekeeping is all about and you will often meet very grateful people and drink lots of tea. Importantly, when you arrive at such a venue, take control, and give at least the impression that you know what you are doing. Make sure you ask permission before ripping people's houses to pieces – I was once sent a bill!

Now what do you do with the bees? The key word is 'isolation'. If you have another site, or a friend with a site he may lend you, or even better, a beekeeper looking for a swarm, you have little problem. If you are able to borrow some hive parts, or make one up from your spares, hive the bees away from home to avoid bringing in disease and then watch them closely. You may be fortunate, they may be relatively clean bees and have a good nature and although it may be late in the season, they may do well enough to support themselves through the coming winter. In the spring, you, or a friend, will have a nice addition to their apiary; even better, you may have converted someone to beekeeping and later, they may return all your loaned equipment, cleaned and sterilized with even perhaps a 'little something' as a thank you!

THE TROUBLE WITH SWARMS

I was called one day to take a swarm, and when I arrived the householder said, 'Oh, a different man today. The other swarm was taken by a nice man from the next village. I called him but he was out and his wife said someone else would come soon.' My colleague had taken the prime swarm, the first and largest swarm to leave a hive. This was a smaller swarm, most likely from the same hive and indicating that the hive would soon 'swarm out' – that is, the hive would issue a repeated number of swarms over a period of days until there were very few bees remaining. I took the swarm by simply 'shaking' them into a cardboard box. I had no spare accommodation so called the colleague who had taken the prime swarm. The old queen was with the prime swarm which he had housed. We disposed of the old queen and later united the two swarms. The next day we again had a call to the same location: the same tree and another small swarm. This we took and another colleague housed them some miles away in a nuc. Eventually the virgin queen emerged and was mated and the colony was passed onto another beekeeper who was just starting out and had no bees. Eventually we discovered the source – an elderly beekeeper a few doors away kept just one hive, for company, as he later told us. He had been confined to hospital for some days during which his bees had all but swarmed out. We managed to return most of his original bees, reunited them and he was a very happy man – happy too that he had inadvertently donated a starter colony to a young beekeeper.

THE SHAKEN SWARM

As will be seen in the chapter on disease (page 88), a solution to the problem of European foul brood (as distinct from American foul brood, which results in the complete destruction of the bees and the hive) is the shaken swarm. Prepare a clean brood box and frames of foundation together with a clean floor and stand them near to the infected hive. Move the infected hive and place the new unit in its place, then simply remove all the frames from the infected hive and shake all the bees into the new clean unit, ensuring you have the queen. Afterwards remove all the infected items away – frames are best burned but the brood boxes can be sterilized and re-used later.

You will, of course, lose all your brood and stored honey but better that than lose the bees; put them on a feeder and they will eventually recover. At the time of writing, a six-frame nucleus of clean bees can cost upwards of £200 so it makes economic sense for the cost of a set of frames of foundation. If in any doubt as to the nature of the disease, as always, contact your nearest bee inspector. From past experience he may even help you to shake the swarm if all is prepared in advance.

CHAPTER 7

HONEY

This chapter examines the nature of honey, how it is made, and the different methods of extraction and production. The honey referred to here is only that produced by the honey bee *Apis mellifera*. Honey or – more accurately – stored nectar, as kept by bumble bees, is completely different.

In the hive, bees use their honey stomachs to ingest and regurgitate the nectar brought in by the flying worker. This process is repeated a number of times as the nectar is passed from bee to bee on its journey from the forag-ing bee to the honeycomb, where it is stored in a changed state caused by the ingestion of enzymes from the honey stomachs of these bees. However, it still has too much water content to be sealed for storage. The bees use their wings to create a draught of warm air throughout the hive and the excess moisture is drawn off. If you stand downwind of a busy hive during the honey flow you will smell the delicious aroma of the honey ripening. Once the excess water has evaporated, the bees will seal each cell with a thin layer of wax, or wax and propolis; once sealed and kept warm and dry it has a very long storage life.

Honey is a mixture of sugars and other compounds; it consists of about 39 per cent fructose, 30 per cent glucose, 1 per cent sucrose and about 10 per cent other sugars such as maltose. The remainder is made up of water (17 per cent) and other elements, including some compounds which are valuable antioxidants and some vitamin C. The composition varies with the type of flowers the nectar came from. On average, 100g of honey has about 300kcal of energy.

THE HARVEST

For most beekeepers the honey harvest is the long-awaited result of a year's work, and for many it is a measure of their success or other-

---

Cell construction

If you examine the cells in the honey-comb in a cut-through section, you will see that the cells slope slightly to the back. The bee fills from the back but when the viscous but liquid honey reaches the front of the cell, the bee starts to construct a sort of dam of capping along the base. As the honey is filled behind this dam, the dam is raised to contain it until eventually it is filled right to the roof of the cell and the capping is completed, ensuring that the cell is full and has no air in it.

A frame full of sealed honey. (Courtesy The Food and Environment Research Agency, Crown Copyright.)

wise. You hear the pride in the voices of those claiming they had so many pounds of honey from each hive, and see the pleasure in their eyes as they tell of the quality of the final product – and rightly so for it is no mean achievement, against all the odds, battling perhaps with inclement weather, perhaps beset with disease problems, almost certainly avoiding the annual problems of swarming. To come to this day and have achieved a crop of honey is something to take pleasure in. But the wise beekeeper will keep his own counsel and take each claim with just a little pinch of the proverbial.

Does the claimant tell you, for example, how many pounds of syrup he had to feed his bees? Will he explain how he imported expensive mated queens to improve his chances? And most importantly, will he tell you how much, or little, of the precious honey he left for the bees for their over-wintering (as he will therefore certainly have to invest heavily in time and money feeding sugar solution for many days to replace what he has taken)?

Never one to spoil the fun, the wise will congratulate and move on, since the mark of a good beekeeper is not calibrated by the size of his honey harvest but by many other factors, not least of which is the health and vigour of his colony.

Pollen storage

Examine a frame packed full of pollen and note the variety of colours from different plant sources. The worker bee mixes a little honey with the pollen loads, then rams it into the cell tightly (using its head!) to remove any air spaces.

Comb packed with pollen; note the varied colours, indicating different flower sources.
(Courtesy The Food and Environment Research Agency, Crown Copyright.)

Nevertheless the day has arrived and there is an air of expectancy as you, and perhaps a friend or two, prepare to take whatever bounty your bees have in store for you. Once again, preparation is everything. The room where you intend to extract the honey must be bee-proof: they object to you taking the honey, will find it with ease if close by and will make every effort to reclaim what is theirs.

If you have borrowed an extractor, have it cleaned and ready. It should have been cleaned by the previous user, unlike one I witnessed, covered in dead bees and grubs – not the sign of a benevolent beekeeper, but the sign of a robber. The honey tank should also have been cleaned and thoroughly dried. Water is the enemy of honey: in its pure form honey will last forever; add water and it will spoil very quickly. The bees know this only too well.

The cost of special de-capping tools is best shared by your beekeeping society.

To remove the cappings from the sealed comb, a simple, strong, long-bladed kitchen knife is adequate, and with care you will lose little.

Of food-quality jugs, funnels and measures, you can never have enough. You should always have too many jars, however! Better a disappointed optimist than odd jugs and containers of honey open to the air awaiting the loan of a few jars. You will also need labels, seals, a marker pen or two, some clean cloths and, most importantly, a huge supply of hot water. It is all a lovely process and much fun but a little honey goes a long way, and it will stick to everything. Hot water is essential to keep everything clean. Make your final check, perhaps with the help of a fellow experienced beekeeper, don your protective clothing, light the smoker and let the fun commence.

The previous evening, remove the queen excluder and insert a clearer board under the supers. The clearer board is simply a crown board fitted with Porter bee escapes, to ensure the bees will have vacated the super. Now all we need to do is lift off the supers and carry them home. Hopefully they will be heavy, and a wheelbarrow lined with a large cloth will make life easier. Do cover them all with more cloth; it may not stop the bees following you but it will stop them getting to their honey! Leave the clearer board for now, replace the roof and exit quietly. The day after you have taken the honey, you will return, remove the clearer board and put back the now emptied supers; the bees will swiftly remove any last vestige of honey and take it down to store.

Safely in the honey room, provided you have not let the supers bounce in the wheelbarrow, you should now be able to examine the harvest. If you have been fortunate, all the super frames will be of capped honey; that is, the bees have ripened it by reducing the water content and then covered it with a cap of wax. You may find, particularly on the outer frames, that they have not yet done so and the cells will contain uncapped and therefore possibly unripe honey. To extract too much of this will spoil the crop and is not worth the risk. However, the bee frequently leaves cells of ripened honey uncapped for ready use. It is dangerous to make hard and fast rules but if more than 10 per cent of a

A simple table-top honey extractor.

frame is uncapped, it is better to give it back to the bees.

Stand your uncapping knife in a jug of very hot water to warm it. Stand the frame upright on a tray, then, having first dried the warmed knife, gently slice off all the cappings so they fall onto the tray. Turn the frame and repeat on the other side, then place the uncapped frame in your extractor. Repeat until either the extractor is full or you have treated all the capped frames.

If you have not sufficient to fill the extractor, ensure you have loaded them in a balanced way or the vibration will make things difficult. Firmly fit the extractor lid and commence to rotate the frames. On machines fitted with an electric motor, the speed can be varied; begin quite slowly and permit the speed to build as the honey is thrown from the spinning frames. Manual machines fitted with a handle on top should be handled in the same way (you may need a friend to take over as it can be tiring, particularly if the honey is thick). Eventually the centrifugal force will have thrown out all the honey. Do not be tempted to use excessive speed in order to obtain the last honey, as you may damage the combs – better to give it back to the bees once you have taken your share, since they are the experts at cleaning out the comb.

If you have more than one loading of the extractor, draw off each batch through the honey gate at the bottom into your honey tank before extracting the next batch. Close the gate and wipe off any drips with a clean finger, time for a taste!

Once you have extracted all the honey and it is all stored in the honey tank, you must permit the contents to settle. The honey will contain many air bubbles and these must be permitted to rise before you start to bottle the product. If the room is warm, leave it overnight.

The cappings can be placed in a square of clean muslin and hung to drip into a container; once they are drained they can be

Food-grade plastic honey bucket or settling tank. Note the large gate valve.

added to your wax collection and rendered down for later use.

Now comes the hard part: thoroughly clean every utensil not required with hot water, dry with sterile cloths and lastly clean the floor and all work surfaces. The extractor may now be returned if you have borrowed it, or handed to the next person requiring it, and it is simply good manners to pass it on in a clean condition. It is also wise to leave the honey room clean, for domestic harmony and because there are small winged creatures outside that can smell honey from miles away and will be eager to investigate as soon as possible.

As soon as your honey has settled in the tank it is time to fill the jars. You will of course have them clean, dried and ready. If you have only a small quantity of honey and merely wish to preserve some for your own consumption, or perhaps as gifts for friends and family, there is no problem with the type of jar you use. (Do not forget your under-standing neighbours with this 'largesse' – it goes a long way to keeping them on your side.) Old jam jars are ideal; wash them thoroughly as you collect them during the year, and just before using them for honey, put them through the dishwasher without a tablet or rinsing fluid to avoid any taint. The very hot water will ensure they are as clean as possible and they should be permitted to dry in the machine where there is little chance of any spores in the air landing on them. Try to avoid using any type of drying cloth for the same reason; remember, this jar will be filled with food and to seal in with it potential sources of mould or bacteria would not be good.

Before bottling you will notice a coating on top of your settling tank, like a pale coloured scum. This is perfectly edible and simply caused by the bubbles of air rising from the honey and bursting on the surface; however, it may spoil the appearance of the finished product. To deal with this you need a warmed dry spoon and a thick slice of freshly baked bread. Carefully skim off the layer without disturbing the honey if you can, and spread the skimmed material on the fresh bread. If you don't know what to do with it now, call me and I will show you. This is heaven!

If the clear honey remains in a warm room it will remain clear, but if stored in cool conditions the honey will almost certainly granulate. This is a process whereby the honey grows small crystals around minor impurities and becomes an almost solid and opaque block. It still retains all of its nutrient qualities and is perfectly acceptable but many people prefer the clear honey, or at least a honey that can be spread or spooned onto their food.

Commercial honey producers avoid this by a number of methods. The first is by fine filtration: under pressure the warmed honey is forced through a fine filter, removing any fine particles upon which the crystals would grow. Unfortunately this reduces the nutrient value of the product and heat treating or sterilizing the honey reduces it even further.

The value of our home-grown product, and one of its major selling points, is that it is a natural product with all the associated health benefits that have long been known to accompany it. If you have honey which has granulated, all is far from lost – you can of course still sell it as it is, and it is now called 'set' honey. However, if you are able to detect the start of the crystallization process, the honey can be removed from the jars and beaten to a creamy consistency before putting it back into clean dry jars. There are honey creamers commercially available but if your quantities are small a hand beater will suffice. This method, in effect, reduces the size of the crystals and prevents them from getting larger and setting completely. The honey now has a creamy white colour and can be marketed as 'creamed honey', still the real deal, still containing all its valuable components and now able to be spread or spooned.

CUT COMB

Cut comb honey is very popular and certainly looks wonderful if presented well. The whole comb is consumed and there are many devotees who consider this the most natural way

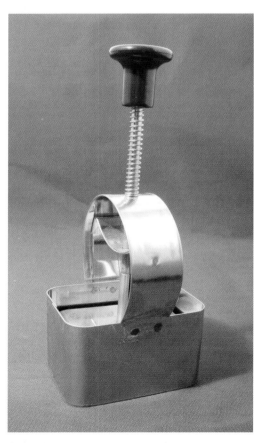

Cutter for cutting out blocks of honeycomb from unwired frames. (Courtesy E.H. Thorne (Beehives) Limited.)

to enjoy honey. Many people appreciate being able to see that the product is fresh from the hive and cannot possibly have been adulterated or processed in any way, and it looks as good as it tastes. To produce this you have to think a long way ahead: the supers on which you intend to encourage the bee to store her honey must first be fitted with frames of unwired foundation or section racks. The use of unwired foundation permits the use of a comb cutter in order to remove evenly shaped blocks of comb.

As these frames must be completely filled, you may wish to consider just a few frames in the centre of the super. These will almost certainly be filled first and more completely, and the remainder of the frames can be fitted with wired foundation and extracted in the normal manner.

Place the filled comb flat on a clean surface, for preference a plastic chopping board retained for the purpose in order that it cannot taint the honey. Use a special comb cutter, which is rather like a steel pastry cutter shaped square in section and much deeper. Remove the block of comb and place it in a special plastic box sold for the purpose and place it on your weighing scales, then top up the box with liquid honey until the weight is correct. Finally, seal it with the 'snap-on' clear plastic lid provided, add an attractive label and the product is ready for sale. Any large but uneven blocks of comb can be carefully removed with a sharp knife and placed in standard honey jars; once again, top up the jar with liquid honey to the correct weight, seal and label. This can now be marketed as 'chunk honey'.

The reason this product sells at a premium is not merely because of the extra value implied by the product, it has much to do with the cost to the beekeeper. With extracted honey you retain the drawn combs for future use. As explained earlier, it takes many pounds of honey to produce a pound of wax and you are selling the wax; add to this the cost of the special boxes and it starts to make economic sense. Comb cutters, like many items, can be borrowed from a friend or your society, and as with all equipment, it should be cleaned thoroughly before returning.

SECTION HONEY

As distinct from cut comb, this is produced by the use of special section boxes. They are fitted in a frame within the super and in essence, the bees draw out comb within the boxes and fill them with honey. The section boxes are then removed, cleaned of any external brace comb or propolis and sold in special packaging. They look very attractive and command a premium. Many customers like them because they are a complete sealed unit prepared by the bee alone, untouched by human hand and they make a very acceptable gift. The difficulty with producing section honey is that bees are generally reluctant to use them and it takes some experience to get them to do so. Also, like selling cut comb, you are losing beeswax which is more costly, in bee terms, to produce than honey. The section boxes and racks can be obtained from your local bee equipment supplier along with the packaging to ready the product for sale.

SINGLE FLOWER HONEY

This is not strictly speaking a different type of honey, merely one that has emanated from a single source. There are those amongst us who are able to detect and enjoy a particular flavour of honey, and there are many – orange blossom, acacia and so on. Many originate from flowering trees, my own favourite being the lime tree. For the beekeeper this demands a high level of expertise and not a little time. To identify the source of the nectar being worked during the season may not be too difficult, particularly if it is local, but this is only the beginning. One has to mark the frames in the super being filled to identify the product later, then mark again when this source stops. There may be only a few frames of each type of honey and they must be extracted separately, a time-consuming business. I am in awe of those who have the time and expertise to do this; for most of us, our honey is a mixture of many types of honey. However, if you have the time and inclination it can be very rewarding. Once again try to befriend a bee society member who does this, he or she may initially be reluctant to share their secrets with you but most will be only too happy to do so.

What you will certainly observe when uncapping your frames prior to extraction is that there is a difference in colour of some honey frames; a start can be made by noting down the number of complete frames that display this change in colour. It is due to the range of different plants and trees from which your bees have foraged during the season and may indicate if there will be a reasonable return from identifying the source in future seasons. Taste a sample of each colour before you extract, this will also help you to appreciate that honey is not just honey but has distinct and identifiable flavours. It's a hard job but someone has to do it!

HONEY FOR SALE

Producing honey with a view to selling it is a different matter and we must consider the presentation of the product and the regulations that exist in order that you can sell it. Some years ago it was sufficient to put the product in a clean jar with a well-fitting lid,

Honey for sale. (Courtesy Rupert Stephenson.)

label it as honey and offer it for sale. This is no longer sufficient – the quantity in the jar must be accurate and stated on the label, and there are now regulations requiring us to indicate the batch number, which you must record as relating to the season it was produced, and a 'Best by' date. Having previously stated that honey correctly ripened and stored will keep almost indefinitely, we must advise the potential customer of the date by which he is advised to use the product. Once again, bee equipment manufacturers sell labels which can be printed to your exact requirements at a cost; they also sell a standard label which they change each season giving a reasonable sell-by date. You must also purchase tamper-proof strips to seal the jar in order to prove that nothing has been added to the product since the original bottling. Ensure the lids are really secure and give the jar a final polish before marketing it; as I stated earlier, a little honey goes a long way and the look of the jar will be ruined by sticky deposits to which dust will cling. As a matter of interest, I am at present using honey I bottled in 1986 and it is still perfect.

OTHER USES FOR HONEY

Honey has long been valued for its medicinal, healing properties and research has shown it is indeed a valuable commodity. Many hospitals now use honey as a wound dressing or salve. The honey keeps the air from the wound and stops the dressing sticking to it. It also reacts with the wound to create a natural antiseptic which aids healing. One of the best honeys for this purpose is called Manuka honey, which is honey made from the nectar of the flower of the Tea Tree, itself known to have antiseptic properties. However, all honeys will serve in a similar way.

Minor digestive problems can be eased by the simple expedient of a spoonful of honey; no one has yet heard children complain of the 'nasty medicine' and there is some evidence that a spoonful of honey can aid problems such as colitis. For sore throats, simply mix in the juice of a freshly squeezed lemon with a spoonful of honey and drink slowly. The ancient method of easing symptoms of a cold included this mixture with an added measure of whisky – although I cannot vouch for the value of the whisky, the value of the honey was well recorded. As a lip balm for sore, dry or chapped lips, mix equal parts of honey and Vaseline in a small container and apply as required; if mixed in small amounts you can put a quantity in a small container and carry it with you in pocket or handbag. I found this very valuable when hill walking, and many friends I walked with were converted to it in preference to commercial products.

Used as a moisturizer, honey works by the same process as a healing balm, the honey reacting gently with the skin and forming a natural antiseptic, and moisturizing the skin. Rub gently into the face and neck and leave in place as a pack for a few minutes before rinsing off well. As a facial scrub, add a small quantity of rolled oats to act as an exfoliant, rub gently into the skin for a few minutes, then leave on for a further five minutes or so before rinsing off thoroughly. There is some evidence that this mixture can help with acne or other minor skin blemishes.

This same mixture can be used to good effect to deal with dry skin on the feet or hands. Use the mixture as a scrub first to exfoliate and remove the dry skin, then leave it in place for five minutes to allow the honey to moisturize the newly exposed skin. Mix the scrub fresh each time you use it as it will not keep more than a few days, although both the constituents will, if kept separate.

Minor burns, grazes, wounds and even sunburn can be soothed and healed faster by the application of a film of honey and there is medical evidence that it helps burns to heal faster with less scarring. I must add a word of caution however, for obvious reasons: carry out all these treatments inside a closed room in the summer or you may attract unwanted visitors of the flying variety.

One can make honey soap and hand cream, well known to be effective and if you are able to produce a suitable product it may be a way to add value to the products you offer for sale. However, within the scope of this book I am trying to keep things simple. Try adding a measure of honey to an equal part of liquid soaps and use as part of your daily beauty routine. And just in case the male readers feel left out, try honey as an aftershave balm to soothe any soreness – I can attest that it works.

CHAPTER 8

WINTERING YOUR BEES

After a busy season, this will be the time when you can take a well-earned rest; the bees will have settled in for the winter and there will be little to see or do. Bees will take occasional flights on a mild and bright day but generally only to defecate or fetch water. Very occasionally they will visit winter-flowering plants, but in general they are in hibernation mode.

However, this is the very time of year that can dictate the results of the coming season; the bees are still alive and still need the occasional visit. There should be no more inspecting of hives – this would be a disaster as the sudden chill could cause irreparable harm – but let us examine the tasks for this period.

WINTER FEEDING

A more accurate phrase would be 'feeding for the winter': if you discover during the dark days that your bees have run out of food, it is almost too late. It is better to feed them as soon as you have taken the honey and they have cleaned up the emptied honey supers. This will give them a good supply to last the winter and you can leave nature to take its course.

Having taken your honey and permitted the bees to clean up the drawn frames, you should have now reduced the hive to a brood box, or double if you intend keeping them like that, a crown board with mesh over the apertures and a roof. The bees will be aware that there is little honey available, although if you have timed it right they will still have some late nectar to gather (from ivy flowers, for instance) and be fairly active. The queen will be laying far fewer eggs and thus much less brood will be developing. The space they previously occupied can now be profitably filled with winter stores.

Feeding them now is important and feeding fast is even more so. If we put on a feeder of two-to-one sugar solution (two parts sugar dissolved in one part water by volume), and constantly keep topping it up, the bees may well misinterpret this as a honey flow, the queen will be induced to lay more eggs and the resultant brood will hatch in the coldest part of the year. They will be a drain on the stores in the hive and eventually many will starve. There is on the market a device called a fast feeder or Ashforth feeder, essentially the size of the hive and about 4 inches deep with a sealed bottom except for a space along one side covered with a strip of glass; it has a bottom bee space and many bees can quickly come up through the hive and take the feed with which you fill the feeder. It takes a lot of feed, around two gallons, but usually one or two fillings are sufficient to restore the hive for the winter. The sugar mixture should be as strong as possible: use hot water and dilute as much sugar into it as it will take. Allow it to cool to blood heat and pour it in. Within twenty-four hours you will observe that the bees have taken it all. Add a little more and if it does not go within the next twenty-four hours, then remove it altogether and close up the hive.

Once again you may be able to borrow a fast feeder from your bee society or a colleague may lend you one; no-one should require one for more than a few days. Alternatively, if you are only intending to 'top up' existing stores in the hive, use a standard bowl type feeder. This has a central cup over a moulded 'volcano', as I call it. Use an empty super or dummy super to give the space you require. The bees come up to lap the sugar and the cup prevents them from escaping. Once again, the same strength feed and no more than two or three days' feeding. Very often you will find the first batch goes very quickly then the next more gradually, usually a good sign that they have had enough. Never leave the feeder on too long even if the bees are not taking the syrup, as it will attract mould. This short period of rapid feeding will ensure that the bees do not start to re-activate the queen into laying and, once complete, the hive should settle for the winter.

If the winter is harder and longer than anticipated, or you have got it wrong, all is not lost. During the winter, if you believe the hive to be running out of stores, you can give the bees a block of bee candy. This is a solid mass of sugar, much like the candy sugar mice are made of, and it contains little water so will cause no harm. It comes in a plastic tub; simply remove the lid and invert the whole thing over the central hole in the crown board (first remove the mesh!). The bees will take this only as they need it, preferring

nectar when it returns, and you can be sure they will not starve. When the spring returns, remove whatever is left and re-seal the lid, keep it in a dry place and it is ready for next year. Mark it with the hive number you previously used it on in case of disease. I confess to a weakness of putting one on all my hives at Christmas – well, we all like Christmas presents!

Also on the market are special formulations of spring feeds. Low in water and high in sugars with some natural added protein to simulate pollen, a hive short of food from the winter will respond better when fed with these substitutes.

Finally, by far the cheapest option and practised by many commercial keepers, place an unopened paper bag of sugar briefly in water, then put the bag over the crown board hole with an empty plastic container over it to prevent bees escaping, and leave them to it. They will chew through the paper to get to the sugar. In the spring you may think it has been snowing with the area covered in chewed up sugar bags! What is important is that the bees have sufficient food at all times. Even when the first sunny days of spring show bees flying from the hive, there may not be food available and a hive having extra demands by the early raising of brood is most likely to fail at this time. A little help now will bring rewards later.

Having fed the bees sufficiently we should now close up the hive. You may wish to use a quilt on top of the crown board to help keep in the warmth, as this is porous and permits ventilation. You may also decide to fit an extra deep-sided roof to stop it lifting in a gale, and many beekeepers place a number of bricks on top to make sure. However, there are special straps available for this purpose – they go over the roof, down each side and under the stand, locking the whole thing together (useful also if you ever intend moving your hive as it prevents movement).

Next, the entrance: you will have put in place your smallest hive block reducing the entrance to almost a single bee size. Consider also a mouse guard, a simple metal strip with a small entrance hole that covers the hive block and prevents rodents chewing their way in. Should a mouse do so it will cause havoc in the frames, eating bees and comb alike. Even if the bees do respond and eventually kill it the damage will be enormous.

Suitably prepared, the hive can now be left for the long nights of the winter but a regular visit should still be made to ensure all is well from the outside. The bee will not need to venture out; their diet, mainly of honey, means there is little faecal matter in the gut and they can survive for fairly long periods without the need to defecate. The hive temperature will fall and the bees cluster around the queen.

Long before you think it is spring, the queen will start to lay a few more eggs, sometimes just a few each day but gradually increasing. Remember that the hive has to be thinking 21 days ahead, the time it takes to raise new brood, so by early February the egg production will have increased and on fine days a few bees may be flying, mainly to collect water, but if it is available they will collect pollen from early plants (winter aconites, pussy willow and hazel). If you observe them bringing pollen to the hive then it is a sure sign of brood-raising and time for you to plan for the spring. If you observe a number of dead bees near to the entrance on the ground, do not be too alarmed – it could well be just spring cleaning and removing bees that have not survived the winter. If, however, the number of dead bees appears to be excessive or some are trying to crawl or stagger about, suspect trouble (*see* Chapter 10).

It is a temptation to ignore the bees in these winter months, especially if you have a distance to travel to your apiary, but it is the opinion of many beekeepers that time spent during these dormant months, ensuring all is well, will pay dividends in the spring. Our aim should be to allow the bees a good clean flying start to the season.

You may read often of the practice of 'hefting' the hive during the winter, that is, by gently lifting the rear of the hive one can estimate whether there is sufficient weight of food within. It takes a lot of experience to do this and it is a rather rough and ready means of assessing the contents, but it is worth a mention. Once again, an experienced member of your local beekeepers' society may offer to demonstrate. For my part I prefer the 'belt and braces' approach and a block of candy on top gives peace of mind.

WINTER TASKS

The long winter months should give you an opportunity to prepare your equipment for the coming season, in particular the cleaning and sterilizing of spare equipment. Your valuable stock of drawn comb should be stacked together and sealed from the wax moth. There are proprietary treatments you can place in the bottom of the sealed stack that will ensure they remain free from any predators and it goes without saying that they must be stored in dry conditions. Spare brood boxes, floors and other wooden parts can be sterilized by the use of a gas blow lamp; give them just enough to start to scorch the wood and melt any propolis or wax that is upon them, paying particular attention to the corners. During this process you will in all probability distort the runners on which the frames rest if they are plastic. It is therefore a good idea to remove them first, and if they are damaged in the process, purchase new ones and re-fit them (they are cheaper than disease!). Alternatively, purchase the galvanized metal version which will last many seasons. Once again, stack the boxes in the dry and cover them to prevent wood-boring insects from taking an interest. The outsides of the boxes can be treated with a non-insecticidal preservative, especially the floors, but not the insides of the boxes.

Time also to peruse the manufacturers' catalogues for items you need for the following season. Wax foundation ordered now, for example, will remain fresh if kept in the manufacturer's packaging and they will thank you for ordering out of season for any items you may require. In the season of writing this, one manufacturer informed me that they have been inundated with their busiest season ever – a very good sign for the bee, but it could result in disappointment for you by delaying your order.

For the amateur woodworkers amongst us, this may also be a perfect opportunity to make some simple additions for our apiary. Floors, for example, perhaps with built-in alighting boards, dummy supers and crown boards are not too difficult for the beginner. Perhaps a decorative or pent roof for your National or other flat-topped hives to enhance their appearance and add an element of individuality. And why not make yourself a five-frame nuc box? So very useful, they rarely need to be out in the elements for more than a week or two at a time so can be manufactured from softwood (give them a good preservative coating) if you cannot manage cedar. I have seen very clever examples with sliding entrance blocks and folding handles; as long as the interior dimensions are accurate, let your imagination run riot. Certain websites have sets of plans to make hive parts for all types of hives. They are very

accurate and can be downloaded and printed off for use in your workshop. Whilst you will never be able to sell such items at a profit – the scale of operation and the use of high-tech precision woodworking machines utilized by the hive manufacturers makes this impossible – there is a great amount of satisfaction to be had in making your own if you are so inclined.

Smoker fuel

Smoker fuel is something you can never have too much of, since it takes up little storage space but can take much time to procure in a busy season. There are many possible fuels: some fellow beekeepers have a pocketful of dry hay and seem to simply stuff some in the smoker from time to time with excellent results. At the other end of the scale are proprietary smoker fuels including small pellets made from wood waste. The standard fuel used to be cartridges made from corrugated cardboard, which gave a good cool smoke and one was usually sufficient for a session of manipulation. Both of these types could be bought from equipment manufacturers. However, with a little planning one can make one's own cartridges. Obtain some corrugated cardboard over the season and store it in the dry (test it to make sure it has not been treated against fire!). Simply roll the cardboard into a cylinder, not too tightly, until it forms a loose fit inside your smoker. The best way to secure the end is with the brown paper glue-backed tape used for parcels. Please do not use plastic sticky tapes of any kind, as it will produce a toxic smoke which may injure the bee, and yourself!

Measure the depth of your smoker box and allow about an inch for the initial balled-up newspaper that you use to light it, and then cut the cylinder into the required length with a small-toothed saw such as a hacksaw.

Do not be tempted to produce your own hay from dried grass mowings; it is very easy when using this to discharge a stream of small burning embers with obvious results, so proper hay from longer dried grass is better. If all else fails you can purchase bags of hay from your local pet shop, although this may be an expensive option. Once again, your local beekeepers' society may come to the rescue if a member has a contact in the farming community – you do not need a large quantity.

CHAPTER 9

MARKETING

Sooner or later your thoughts may well turn to selling your produce, although for many it is as much for the interest as the money. Whatever you make will go towards your annual costs but never be misled into thinking there is a fortune to be made. Importantly, it can add to the enjoyment of your hobby, you will have a measure of the quality of your products by comparison with others and you will meet some interesting people.

One of the first things to decide is where to market your produce. It is unlikely that you will produce enough honey to supply even a small shop as they will require a regular supply of your product to make the exercise worthwhile; having said that, if your area or village still retains an independent shop, they may consider putting a few jars on sale as a local product. Remember, however, that they will rightly expect a profit on each item and this will reduce your share. Stalls at local markets will be the same and it will be unlikely that the amount you have will justify the hire of a stall for the day. Also it may be difficult to secure such a stall on a short-term basis.

It may be worth exploring local 'bring and buy' sales or small craft fairs set up once or twice a year. However, bear in mind once again that your margins will be reduced by the cost of hiring even a small stall and you

will need to calculate selling much of it to offset the cost. If you have priced your product too high or it is just a bad day for it, you could well end up with a loss, which will have to be offset later.

Some beekeeping societies will hold an annual sale of their members' produce and this is a very good idea, as there will be a number of different products on offer as well as honey, such as candles and pollen. One enterprising member made a batch of wooden honey dippers on his lathe and sold the lot in one afternoon. These events are also great opportunities for what we now call 'networking' (we used to call it 'meeting people', but the outcome is the same). Never measure your success by the amount you sell on one afternoon; you will have put not just your produce but yourself on the market and long after the event you may still be reaping the rewards. Many people prefer to do business with someone they know, or whose product has been tried or recommended by a friend, and it is this 'after shock' of business which must be added into your calculations.

The size of the venue and the large quantity and range of products will attract many customers and the society usually charges its members a small amount per table for its own funds. This is also a great opportunity to view the goods on offer by other members, to assess the quality of your own product and give you ideas for future revenue. Often these sales follow the annual honey show and you may even win a small prize as well of disposing of your annual surplus.

Hive manufacturers and equipment suppliers still market the original straw 'skep' specifically for the purpose of advertising your wares – with one of these on display and an attractive arrangement of your produce your product should almost sell itself. It should be a one-off purchase that will last many years but I did hear of someone who was made an offer he could not refuse and sold the skep as well, hopefully at a profit!

Selling from your home with a sign on the gate may well prove profitable if you are prepared to stay at home much of the day and tolerate would-be purchasers turning up at all hours, sometimes long after you have disposed of your surplus.

I have in the past put the produce out on a folding card table in the lay-by outside my home with a large sign indicating the price and a bowl for the money, and have been surprised and delighted when all the produce sold and not one penny was stolen. This was many years ago and I am not sure I would take the gamble again but many producers of fruit, eggs and vegetables as well as honey still do it in rural areas and never have anything stolen.

It is possible to sell produce via the Internet but one would have to have a considerable quantity to cover the costs of postage and packing, as well as the problem of people contacting you long after your produce is sold.

There are strict rules and regulations regarding the sale of food products. No longer can we just put a label on the jar of honey stating its content; we now must have a batch number or 'Best by' date (preferably both), and the weight must precisely match that stated on the label. Fortunately hive and equipment manufacturers sell labels with all the relevant details printed on them and you may be able to borrow scales approved for weighing the jars from your local beekeepers' association (*see* page 72).

Finally, presentation: the purchase of good clear jars of a standard size and shape will do much to sell your product. You must only sell your very best and retain anything not perfect for your own use.

SOME OTHER ITEMS FOR SALE

Of course what follows is not a complete list; attend a local craft fair and you will soon get ideas of your own. Beeswax can be made into many products to sell, apart from the usual candles. Beehive manufacturers sell a vast number of rubber moulds for candles, colourings to tint them and perfumed oils to scent them as well as the wicks and other items you may need. The range of moulds and designs one can achieve is enormous and it can turn into a full-time hobby in its own right.

Your wax scraps will first need to be rendered down. If you have used a solar wax collector (*see* page 28), that wax will be reasonably clean; however, much of the remainder will not be. You will perhaps have used comb and foundation, no longer clean enough to reuse in the hive, scrapings from your regular inspections, and so on.

The method I use to clean it is as follows. You will need a couple of old saucepans (no longer required for the domestic food department – once used for wax they are very difficult to clean sufficiently to satisfy the needs of the cook). The basic principle is to use them as a bain-marie, that is, a saucepan or steel bowl floating in a pan of lightly boiling water.

Moulded beeswax candles. (Courtesy E.H. Thorne (Beehives) Limited.)

Turned cherry wood box finished with home-made beeswax polish.

The reason for this is twofold. Firstly, wax melts below the temperature of boiling water, if raised above this it will darken and dis-colour. The second is fire: raise the tempera-ture too high and the wax will catch fire.

One can of course purchase special equip-ment from the hive manufacturers, essentially the same thing and often with a built-in heater element; however, as the saying goes, you can buy anything if you have enough money and the outlay may not be justified by the reward for the backyard entrepreneur.

Once a year, I place all my wax in one pan with a quantity of water, set the heat on low and bring it all to the boil ensuring all is covered in boiling water. I then turn off the heat and allow it to settle; then, with an old spoon, I skim off any 'scum' on top and allow the mixture to go cold. You will now have a cake of clean wax on top of the contents of the pan, and the water will be underneath. Remove the cake of wax and scrape off the whitish loose matter underneath.

Place the second pan inside the first,

which now has more water in it; bring to the boil, then turn down the heat and permit it to simmer, making sure the bottom pan does not boil dry or your wax will burn. Place your wax inside the second pan and allow it to melt. At this stage you can then pour it into candle moulds or whatever you choose. I tend to pour this into smaller home-made moulds, the foil 'cups' some small cakes and pies are sold in, so that I now have a supply of small blocks of wax and do not have to melt down the whole lot for smaller projects. To release the wax from the moulds, after they have set, simply stand them in the freezer overnight and the next morning they will fall out.

Having religiously saved all your scraps of wax and rendered them down in a clean and presentable fashion, beehive manufacturers will offer to buy it from you, or exchange it for an agreed amount of new foundation. This is usually a good deal for the beekeeper as it reduces your costs. However, the manufac-turers reserve the right to refuse any wax they consider tainted with residues of certain medications. It is perhaps this wax that is best converted into other items for sale. You may wish to turn your surplus wax into furni-ture polish, a very valuable commodity. For my own part I could never use wax for candles as I deem it far too valuable and prefer to keep it for my other love, woodwork-ing. Made essentially from pure beeswax and pure gum turpentine (not turpentine substi-tute, which is white spirit), the polish is the best possible treatment for real wood.

The following simple recipe also uses up those odd scraps of soap left from the bar in the bathroom. To 4 ounces of beeswax add 1 ounce of white candle wax and enough soap scraps to fill a teacup. Place in your bain-marie with one pint of pure turpentine and a quarter of a pint of water, heat until all the ingredients are thoroughly dissolved and pour into tins.

Safety note: beware of using a gas ring for this as the mixture when warm is very inflammable. Use an electric ring, keep the heat as low as required just to melt the contents and always have a fire blanket to hand when you carry out this operation.

There are many recipes for furniture polish and you may wish to experiment until you obtain a mixture that suits you and your customers.

One can obtain suitable tins and labels from your local beekeeping equipment manufacturer, as a marketing ploy they look so much better than odd containers. Consider also a small mould to make sticks of pure beeswax, once again, very popular with woodworkers and wood turners. Have you ever had a 'sticky' drawer in your house? Simply rub both runners with a stick of pure beeswax and the problem is solved.

COSTS AND HOW TO REDUCE THEM

Perhaps this is the best place to discuss cost, not just of your produce but indeed the whole enterprise. As I said earlier, it is very unlikely that you will ever make a real profit but the sale of some produce may assist in offsetting your annual costs. If you sit down and list all your costs you will soon begin to realize the truth of those words and I would not like either to mislead anyone or even to attract a would-be beekeeper whose only motivation is profit.

First to your product: it is fairly simple to calculate the cost of the jar and label and the seal for the lids, but very difficult to asses the cost of all your equipment over the period. Even if you spread them over a number of years you still have to consider annual expenditures on sugar syrup, medications and replacement parts.

Purchased new, a hive is a very expensive item, because the timber it is fabricated from is expensive, as are the precision machines required to manufacture the hives. If you take the time and effort to make your own to the correct specification, as I have, you will be astounded at just how many hours it takes and there is also the waste if you make any mistakes in the building – there is no place for wood filler on a bee hive. At current prices a new hive such as a National will cost in the region of £250 or more but, of course, this cost can be spread over many seasons. You would need to be very fortunate to produce and sell enough to cover even these costs let alone all the other costs as mentioned.

Finally we must consider labour costs and this is where things can get very scary. Probably the best way to deal with that is the answer given concerning the realities of growing vegetables in a book I read long ago. A friend of the author of the book was having a discussion with him over a drink in the local hostelry about the real cost of growing a cabbage – seed, compost, fertilizer, not to mention the hours of labour to produce it. The friend told the author, in very scathing tones, that it was cheaper to buy his cabbage at the supermarket and devote his spare time to playing golf. The author answered, 'But what profit is there in a game of golf?' And that surely must be the point: if you get pleasure from your beekeeping, if you enjoy the challenge of keeping bees and the companionship of other beekeepers and gain pleasure out of selling a few items, does it really matter? To reduce everything to a matter of pounds and pence is rather sad; better by far to enjoy the hobby.

CHAPTER 10

DISEASES

One has of course to be aware of the diseases that beset the bee in order that action can be taken to prevent them or to deal with them once identified. Since I first became interested in bees the problem and range of diseases has become somewhat more complex, but the reader will I hope forgive me for not making too great an issue of it. The first book on gardening I was given as a child had such a large and off-putting chapter on pests and diseases that I was almost dissuaded from what has become a lifelong interest. I say 'almost' because over many years I have been grateful for the information that book contained. Experience has taught me that you would be extremely unfortunate to suffer many of these diseases; you should nevertheless be aware of them.

There are some ailments which all beekeepers will learn to live with for the foreseeable future, there are some that good management and regular treatment can avoid, and there are some recent problems which still present something of a mystery – no doubt time and research will give us some answers. In the introduction to this book I expressed the wish that as many people as possible should keep bees, to try to preserve colonies of these wonderful creatures while they and we attempt to uncover the problems that beset them. Surely if more people keep bees, then

more intelligent questions will be posed for answers that science will provide? And perhaps you will be the individual to supply the one piece of vital evidence that solves some of the mysteries.

Finally I make an abject apology if I have missed something, some locally known remedy or preventative. I have spoken to as many beekeepers as possible and included some of their remedies and interesting devices, but the scope of this book is not large enough to include everything. It remains a book to encourage the would-be beekeeper and I hope nothing in the following chapter does anything to dissuade them.

PREVENTION

It would be unrealistic to believe that any creature is free from the possibility of disease; when there was an abundance of wild colonies, they too fell prey to diseases, some of which were capable of wiping out the colony. However, as with all creatures that man chooses to domesticate, we must take some responsibility for exacerbating the situation. Moving colonies from location to location, swapping equipment and hive parts and introducing parts of one colony into another, all have an impact on the spread of ailments. As will be seen later, it is known that some ailments are amplified by inducing stress in the bee; the disease may well be present but lies dormant until a level of stress induces the disease to take hold. And stress can even be induced by too frequent investigation and manipulation of the hives. With our small colonies, and some good management, we plan to avoid stress at all costs.

Cleanliness is all-important: your hive tool, manipulating cloth and even your gloves can transfer problems from one hive to another. It may be a simple matter to sterilize the former with the flame from a small gas blowlamp between colonies. A spare set of manipulating cloths will be cheaper to obtain or make than the cost of treating disease, and they can be washed and sterilized with a proprietary disinfectant in between visits. A spare pair of gloves is always useful and to change them between visits is no hardship; they too can be sterilized later. Hands too should be considered, the proprietary alcohol-based hand wash is simple and quick to apply, but give your newly cleaned hands a good coating with the smoker afterwards; bees do not like alcohol.

SPOTTING THE SIGNS

The sight of a number of dead bees in front of your hive does not inevitably indicate trouble; as explained earlier, worker bees fly for around six weeks before they wear themselves out. Realistically many will die out in the open, perhaps miles from home, but some will die in the hive, and the efficient workers inside will drag their bodies out and fly a short distance to dispose of them. Some, however, will just fall at the hive entrance. What should cause alarm is a number of bees on the ground below the entrance that seem unable or unwilling to fly. The first sign of a sick bee is that it can no longer fly, as it takes

a lot of energy to do so and this will be the first sign of trouble within.

When manipulating your hive, you may spot signs of trouble. Some diseases cause unusual distortion of the cell cappings or even the cells themselves, and action at this stage may prevent a more serious outbreak or at least avoid spreading the disease to other colonies.

DISEASES AFFECTING THE ADULT BEE

Acarine disease (Acarapisosis woodi)

This *is* caused by a species of tiny mite that enters the 'portholes' through which the bee breathes and takes up residence in the trachea inside where it feeds off the blood of its host. Eventually it will block them and the bee will die, and meanwhile it has passed on mites to other bees in the colony. If untreated, eventually the colony will become much weakened. This pest cannot live long without a bee so hives and frames themselves are not the source of infection; it merely passes from bee to bee. This disease seems more prevalent in Britain and Europe and rare in other parts of the world.

Fortunately it is not common and seems to come and go from time to time. Like all such problems, spot it early and there are some good treatments available, usually consisting of strips impregnated with an acaricide. Trade names are changing all the time, your local bee inspector will advise. (Folbex used to be in use but some older medications have now been outlawed, and some have been superseded by better, or safer ones.)

Nosema (Nosema apis)

This is a common disease and you will

certainly have to learn to live with it. Research has indicated that all honey bees have it in their system and it is one of the diseases that are exacerbated through stress. Often there is no cause that can be placed at the foot of the beekeeper; a poor season or lack of food at the wrong time can trigger an outbreak, but we can do much to help prevent it taking a hold.

The cause is *Nosema apis*, described as a microscopic spore-forming animal living in the gut of the bee and feeding off the contents. It can be passed from one bee to another by them ingesting infected faeces as they do when cleaning the hive. This will occur more frequently during the winter and early spring months due to the fact that the bee will defecate outside during warmer weather. The infection tends to shorten the life of the bee by as much as 50 per cent and it follows that with a flying life of only about six weeks, this will have a disastrous effect on the ability of the hive to collect and store honey and to reproduce. If untreated a colony is severely weakened and apart from the economic loss the whole hive may become unviable. Signs to watch for are a colony that has failed to build up in the spring, or built up very slowly and is unable to gain a sufficient population in time to store sufficient honey. Such a colony may well die out altogether the following spring. Individual bees may be seen crawling about in a very distressed manner and signs of watery faeces in the hive may be present. The only sure way to identify the culprit is under the microscope and a sample of the dead bees should be sent for examination.

There are two main methods of control. The first is by preventing the condition from building up; Fumidil B is an antibiotic which, mixed with the sugar syrup in the autumn, or less effectively in the spring, will reduce the infestation and as there are many months before honey is stored, the substance does not contaminate the honey crop. These antibiotics are not cheap, and later in this chapter we will discuss some other treatments, some home-made, which have stood the test of time as being effective.

The other method of control is by prevention; it follows that to reduce the spread, we need to keep our colony as clean as possible. As discussed in Chapter 4, by progressively working the frames to one side and replacing them with clean new frames from the other side over a period of time, we can put the bees onto new frames and reduce the amount of infection. Changing the brood box, floor and crown board is also a simple matter, they can all be sterilized and replaced later. I cannot stress enough the importance of good hygiene, for the keeper of one or perhaps two hives it is a simple matter, one of routine which once adopted will become second nature.

Amoeba

Amoeba are often found in bees that have Nosema but it does not infest on anything like the same scale. Should you have to send your bees for analysis, the report will often mention them but they rarely cause problems on their own and will be controlled by the medication for Nosema.

Paralysis

The cause of this distressing condition is thought to be a virus living within the tissues of plants and there are various strains of the condition showing differing symptoms. The bees may appear crawling or lying in an unnatural position, and their wings may be held at awkward angles. They may appear to be shivering and sometimes display a darker colour than the rest of the colony. Unfortunately, viruses do not respond to chemical treatments and the best option at present seems to be to re-queen the colony from a strain known to be free of this condition.

BROOD DISEASES

Having now dealt with the diseases of the adult bee we come next to diseases of the brood. We begin with the two most destructive.

American foul brood (Bacillus larvae)

At the time of writing, this is sadly on the increase. There seems to be no cure and Government legislation has deemed that, if identified, the colony and hive must be destroyed by burning and the ashes buried. The cause is the spores of *Bacillus larvae*, which are almost impossible to destroy. If not dealt with they can be transferred to other hives and if it does not kill the colony in the first season, it will certainly do so in the second. As the name suggests, the brood combs smell foul, the cells are sunken and distorted, the larvae become almost like a sticky mess in the cell and the whole comb takes on a dark and sunken appearance. Compare this with the healthy brood and you will quickly see the difference.

A number of chemicals can be used as a preventative, usually put in sugar feed or trickled along the tops of the frames, and these have some merit, but I repeat: there is at present no cure. If you suspect you may have it, contact your local bee inspector without delay. It follows therefore that your frequent inspections are vitally important in order to discover this as soon as possible – you may not prevent the eventual outcome of your colony but could well stop the infection from spreading to other

Brood frame showing infection by American foul brood (AFB); some chalk brood present. (Courtesy The Food and Environment Research Agency, Crown Copyright.)

Frame of healthy brood in all stages; note the drone brood cells at the bottom of the frame. (Courtesy The Food and Environment Research Agency, Crown Copyright.)

European foul brood (EFB) showing sunken appearance and discolouration. (Courtesy The Food and Environment Research Agency, Crown Copyright.)

One essential difference between this and AFB is that all the larvae die before the cell is capped over and closer examination will show they are lying in unnatural positions (perhaps this is why the workers often remove the dead brood). Also, there will not be the same degree of discolouration, just a generally lower appearance of the comb accompanied by the tell-tale smell.

There is a treatment which can be effective if the outbreak is caught soon enough: an antibiotic mixed in sugar syrup; however, in more serious cases, the bee inspector may order the destruction of the colony. Left untreated the disease can spread to other colonies and your own colony will be unable to develop into a viable entity. One way to rescue an infected hive is to put all the flying bees into a clean hive (*see* 'The shaken swarm', page 63).

colonies. Never assume that this is in any way an indication of your competence or otherwise, since the disease can be spread simply by a robber bee visiting from an infected colony miles away and there is little you can do to prevent it. You may well have carried out preventative treatment, but if others have not, then the result is inevitable.

European foul brood

Once again a fairly serious problem but less so than the previous infection. It does not appear as widespread as AFB but seems more localized. The difficulty is in identifying it; very often there are initially few signs and, often, a good colony will remove diseased brood to contain the spread. You may observe a few sunken cells but on the next inspection they may be absent. Once again, if you are in any doubt, consult your bee inspector.

Chalk brood (Ascophera apis)

For many beekeepers this was initially thought not to be a disease at all but just something that happened from time to time. The dead larvae in the cell would take on a strange white appearance; the larva would be loose in the cell and eventually turn black. However, this has now been identified as caused by the fungus *Ascophera apis*. The spores may be brought in by the workers and ingested by the developing larvae. The problem at present is not too serious, since not all the cells are infected and there is no evidence that it can spread from one to the other – the spores have to be ingested. Somewhat localized in nature, until recently it seemed not a serious threat. However, alongside other disease problems in America, it is starting to be recognized as a threat, perhaps a different strain has developed there. While looking for the causes of disappearing colonies, of which more later, they discovered that this condition was on the increase.

Sac brood

Again, this was not a common disease in the past but is starting to increase (or perhaps our greater awareness of problems together with increased education and vigilance of beekeepers has revealed more cases). As the name suggests, the dead larvae are found in a sort of watery sac with their back towards the entrance and their head uppermost. The best guess for the cause is that it may be a genetic mutation and re-queening the hive may be the answer.

Addled brood

It is easy to confuse addled brood with sac brood in some of its forms, and only an expert would be able to tell the difference. It is thought to emanate from a queen defect and the only known solution is to re-queen the colony.

Chilled brood

This is not a disease at all but a result of the young brood receiving insufficient warmth during their growth, often found at the margins of frames where there is less heat.

The cause may be due to poor management on the part of the beekeeper, perhaps giving them more brood than they can cover. Or there may be a sudden loss of bees due to chemical spraying in the area or even due to swarming and leaving insufficient bees to manage, but this is rare. Many dead bees in front of the hive will indicate spraying is the culprit. As distinct from other brood diseases, the dead larvae will tend to be all in a group, at the edge of, or at the bottom of, the comb.

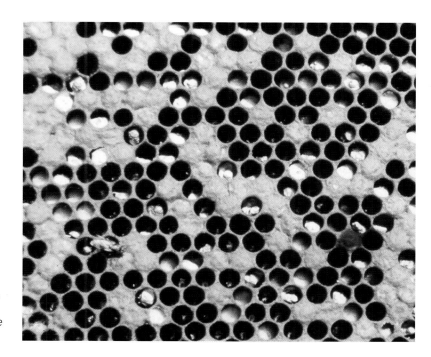

Chalk brood with the distinct white chalk-like appearance of the dead larvae.

Chalk brood mummies on the floor of the hive having been ejected by the workers. (Courtesy The Food and Environment Research Agency, Crown Copyright.)

Adult female Varroa mite by David Crossley, Principal Photographer, FERA (image much enlarged). (Courtesy The Food and Environment Research Agency, Crown Copyright.)

Varroa mite (Varroa destructor)

Varroa mite is the one identified pest that affects both brood and adult bees. The very word strikes fear into many beekeepers, but should not, since there is much that can be done to control it. Great advances have been made in recent years, in both treatment and management, and whilst we may have to live with it, we need not fear it.

Varroa first appeared in the UK in 1992. Originally called *Varroa jacobsoni*, it is now referred to as *Varroa destructor* (Acari: Varroidae). The pest has been present throughout Europe since the late 1970s after being accidentally introduced from Asia where its host is *Apis cerana*, the Asian honey bee. It is an external parasite and effects both brood and adult bees. A small red mite related to the spider family, it can be seen with the naked eye, or a hand lens for those of us with failing sight, and resembles to me a small red crab, round and domed in shape with legs visible on both sides of the 'shell'.

The effect on the bee and in particular the brood is that they fail to fully develop, they appear small and stunted with distorted wings and it follows that a colony badly affected will not thrive and eventually will die out. Also the mite makes the bee more prone to other infections by the simple expedient of introducing viruses though the wounds it inflicts.

The Varroa mite is thought to be responsible for the death of a large percentage of com-

Deformed wings on a worker bee resulting from infestation of Varroa at the larval stage. (Courtesy The Food and Environment Research Agency, Crown Copyright.)

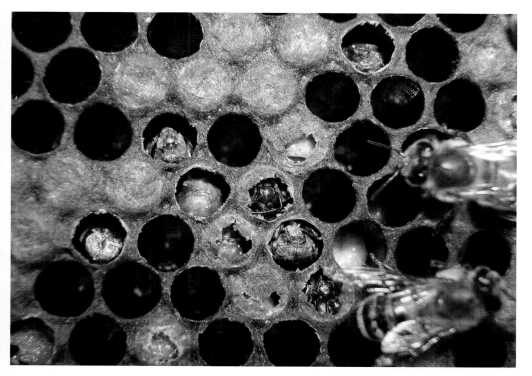

Image showing damage to brood and cells caused by Varroa mite. (Courtesy The Food and Environment Research Agency, Crown Copyright.)

mercially housed bees in the UK and possibly all the feral colonies as well (this alone is a reason why we must strive to keep bees). It is estimated that 35 per cent of the world's food depends on pollinating insects and of these a large percentage are honey bees.

There is not the space in this book to discuss the pest in great detail, but a brief résumé should give an idea of the problem. Varroa cannot move from hive to hive unaided – it depends on the bee to carry it there; by clinging onto the bee it is transferred by robber bees or bees naturally swarming. Even the drone, with his 'pass key' to visit any hive he chooses, will have played a role in the transfer of this pest.

Once in the hive the egg-carrying female mite enters the unsealed brood cells; they appear to favour drone brood cells but also visit the worker cells. The female waits in the brood food until the cell has been capped and within a few days she lays a number of eggs while she starts to feed on the developing bee larvae, using her sharp mouth parts to ingest its blood. These eggs then hatch out and the resultant offspring feed also on the larvae.

After a period of a few days the offspring mate with their sisters and another generation starts. If this mating does not occur the females will be sterile and the male cannot survive outside the cell in any case. The new mites then emerge after the weakened pupae emerge and move on to infest other parts of the hive.

Following the initial fear generated by the arrival of Varroa, a form of treatment was found which had already proved effective in Europe. Strips of a chemically impregnated paper, usually with a pyrethroid and called Bayvarol or Apistan, could be inserted between the frames after the honey harvest. The substance would destroy the mites and the strips could be removed. As frequently happens, the mite has become resistant to these chemicals in some areas and they are no longer so effective.

The outward signs of a severe infestation may be seen in the brood: some larvae will die before emerging or shortly afterwards and will usually be removed by the bees; however, there may be areas of apparently dead brood, damaged cells or deformed bees

Varroa mesh floor. (Courtesy E.H.Thorne (Beehives) Limited.)

Clockwise from top: Tropilaelaps, Varroa, Braula and Mellitiphis on same scale. (Courtesy The Food and Environment Research Agency, Crown Copyright.)

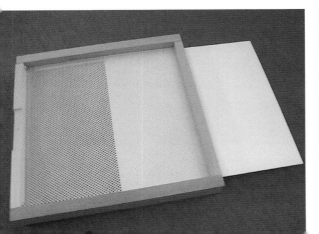

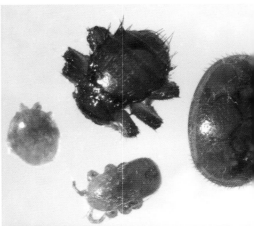

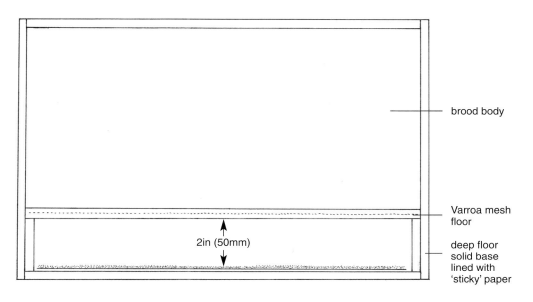

brood body

Varroa mesh floor

deep floor solid base lined with 'sticky' paper

2in (50mm)

Illustration of special deep floor under Varroa mesh floor with wood block.

apparently wandering aimlessly. It is estimated that a vigorous hive can tolerate a low level of infestation without harm; the number of 1,000 is often quoted, and in some states of America they accept a level of 4,000 to 5,000. However, in view of the fact that numbers can rise suddenly, any number should be cause for alarm.

Regular monitoring of the population and subsequent treatment of the hive if the population of mites rises too high is essential: even if the hive seems otherwise normal, there can be an exponential rise in population in the spring and many infected bees will fail to return from foraging. This may also explain sudden bee loss in some cases.

There are many other methods of control for Varroa: some may leave residues in the wax combs; others themselves are dangerous to handle; some are based on essential oils and the vapours they exude. My favourite, and it is tried and tested, involves coating all the bees

in icing sugar! A fine sieve can be purchased or borrowed and put over the brood box, preferably in late autumn as the sugar system will only treat adult bees. A quantity of icing sugar is then scraped over the sieve and permitted to fall onto the bees between the frame, and excess will fall through the Varroa mesh floor. The icing sugar appears to make the mites lose their footing and they fall off and through the Varroa floor where they can be safely disposed of. The reaction is immediate, the bees will not trouble you while you treat them, they are consuming the sugar, and best of all, you are not introducing water into the hive.

The best approach would be to research all the possible cures and treatments via the Internet, and then discuss these with your local beekeepers' society.

Not strictly a method of control, but more an important means of assessing the mite population is the Varroa floor. This is a 3mm mesh floor through which mites and other debris can pass but the bee cannot. Mites are frequently dislodged from the bodies of worker bees in a cleaning action and fall beneath the mesh where they may be unable to return. There will also be dead male mites who have a very short life span once ejected from the cell in which they were raised. The floor beneath the mesh should be lined with a single sheet of stiff paper. This should be inspected at frequent intervals and the number of mites assessed. Once completed, the paper should be removed and burnt and a new liner inserted. A more efficient addition that will improve the capture rate is to coat the paper with a thin layer of Vaseline and cooking oil to make it sticky; this will ensure a complete trapping of any mites.

Several beekeepers have voiced concern at the fact that this floor is open at the rear, and may be visited by other bees on which the mites could hitch a lift. Also, the wax moth will be attracted to the particles of wax fallen there and cause problems. Accordingly some have devised a deeper version of the floor with a greater gap under the mesh, as much as 2 inches (50mm), and have sealed the gap at the rear with a temporary strip of wood. As always the beekeeper is inventive and will rise to any new challenge.

Drone brood removal
So-called 'biotechnical' methods of control are now in use. As the mite favours drone brood for its attacks, the raising and destroying of drone brood before the drones emerge can significantly reduce the level of infestation. By inserting a shallow super fitted with drone foundation underneath, the bees will be encouraged to produce drones. If these are then removed and the drone combs destroyed before they emerge, vast numbers of mites will be destroyed along with them, and the

frames can be re-fitted with drone foundation and re-inserted immediately. There is no infection risk from the frame and the process can then be repeated.

Comb trapping
This is a variation on the drone system: a number of frames are selected and the queen is caged between special frame wires. After a number of days, when the frames are full of sealed brood, the queen is released and the combs, complete with mites, are destroyed.

The major disadvantage with both these systems is that it requires a fairly high level of skill on the part of the beekeeper and also reduces the efficiency of the hive while it is being carried out.

COLONY COLLAPSE DISORDER

In recent months much has been reported in the press of the mystery of the disappearing bees. Various names have been given to this condition: Colony Collapse Disorder is a term commonly used. A previously healthy hive would, within a matter of weeks, suddenly be almost empty. There were no signs of masses of dead bees outside the hive, and the few remaining bees, usually dead, were found not to have any identifiable ailment or infection. These conditions were found in the UK, in the USA and throughout Europe and hive losses of more than 50 per cent were reported by some sources. In America, extensive research indicated that there was no one mystery disease, and no single cause could be determined, so to give it a name was inappropriate. Evidence began to accumulate, however, showing that something was very wrong.

The first piece of evidence came from the bees themselves. Using modern techniques of DNA sampling, the DNA of the bee was removed from the remains of dead bees and the remaining sample analyzed; there were found to be traces of as many as forty different compounds commonly in use as agricultural insecticides and fungicides. None of these compounds was known to cause bee death on its own; all had been thoroughly tested before being approved for use. Also found were traces of a condition known as Israeli Acquired Paralysis Virus, IAPV for short, a sort of AIDS in bees, and this condition is frequently found in bees throughout the world but it appears dormant and normally it does no harm in a healthy bee.

One conclusion some researchers arrived at was that the accumulation of these chemical traces had made the bee more vulnerable to its IAPV burden; weakened by them, the virus became active.

Another theory, more surprisingly, was that this accumulation of pesticides was damaging the bee's ability to navigate when under stress. Quite simply, the workers would fly out to forage, become disorientated and being unable to find the hive would eventually perish. In response the hive would send out more flying bees in an attempt to maintain the hive; these too would fail to return, and over a period of a few weeks, or even days, the colony would be too small to be viable as by multiple swarming out of the workers, the colony would die through starvation. This would explain the absence of dead bees in the immediate vicinity of the hive.

One of the compounds that became a suspect was the new group of neonicotinoids, chemicals designed to be sprayed onto agricultural products at an early growth stage, entering the sap stream of the plant and remaining an effective killer of plant-sucking aphids. Apart from the loss to the plant itself by sucking the sap, the aphids are responsible for the transmission of viral and fungal infections. Traces of these compounds have been discovered in both the pollen and the nectar of the flowering plants and, by this transmission, the bees may have been building up a greater concentration in their system.

As a response to concerns, in the UK the Co-operative Food Society has banned the use of such compounds on any of its food products as well as giving a generous donation to bee research in order to further investigate the problems of bee loss.

In France the beekeepers lobbied their Government in a very demonstrative way, setting fire to empty hives at the gates of the Ministry responsible in order to highlight their plight. They also blamed the increasing use of monoculture in agriculture for reducing the available flowering plants the bees require. As another means of bringing attention to their problem they installed a pair of beehives on the roof of a giant exhibition hall beside the Champs Élysées in 2009 and filled these hives with Buckfast bees! The results were amazing: the hives produced a large amount of honey despite the traffic pollution and remained very healthy.

This is thought in part to be due to the absence of agricultural sprays in the bees' foraging area and the large number of flowering plants and trees in the vicinity. They intend to increase the trial in future.

In Spain, researchers discovered evidence that malnutrition in bees was causing the stress that led to Colony Collapse Disorder. Whatever the cause, it has been identified as the most serious condition facing the honey bee and indeed it is now thought to affect other pollinators. One group of American researchers have theorized that if an answer is not found, the honey bee could disappear by 2035; however, the media love to seize on such situations and there may be a degree of alarmism in the reports.

Frame full of healthy brood. (Courtesy The Food and Environment Research Agency, Crown Copyright.)

Melittiphis **(Melittiphis alvearius)**

This small mite (sometimes called the pollen mite) appears to do no harm to the bee but is merely a scavenger; it tends to feed on pollen that has been stored by the bee. Due to the enzymes that the bee adds to the pollen, it prefers this readily digested food. The mites may appear on your test paper but as the photograph on page 92 shows it is easily distinguished from Varroa, being much smaller, reddish brown, and having six legs.

Braula **(Braula coeca)**

Pronounced 'browler', this is commonly called the bee louse. This is a wingless fly and has probably lived alongside the honey bee for many generations. Braula has a very strange lifestyle: it lives on the honey bee, sometimes in great numbers but most bees have two or three, and by stimulating the bee near its mouth parts the bee is induced to open its mouth and the louse steals some food! It does not appear to cause serious harm. In fact a report from a research institute in Edinburgh suggests that this pest is being destroyed in great numbers by treatment given for Varroa and it may become an endangered species!

Wax moths

There are two varieties of wax moth: the greater and the lesser. This is not a pest of the bee but an insect that will lay eggs in the hive. The eggs hatch and the burrowing young form a number of tunnels through the cappings of comb and often into the comb itself. Severe infestation can necessitate the replacement of whole areas of comb. The moth can enter the hive through any unguarded aperture, and for this reason it is best to have all ventilation holes and holes in crown boards covered with mesh. The adult moths can sometimes be seen hanging under the edges of the roof and they will seek their way in though any space between the roof and the hive in their pursuit of wax.

There is also the real danger of this pest invading stored empty comb and these should be protected with crystals of a benzene compound available from equipment suppliers. This substance is placed in the stored boxes of comb; the fumes rise up though the comb and deter the moth, in much the same way as mothballs are used to keep clothing free of moths. One way of destroying this pest on honey supers is to store the frames in the deep freeze for at least forty-eight hours before thawing out and extracting; this will also kill pollen mites and Braula larvae.

FUTURE THREATS?

The following two pests are not as yet present in the UK but their geographical progress is being closely monitored. (*See* Further Information, page 110 for details.)

Tropilaelaps (Tropilaelaps alvearius)

As stated above, this mite is not yet present in the UK. However, unless the transport of bees and bee products worldwide is stopped, it is almost certain that it will enter the UK. It is almost as destructive as Varroa; the mite is smaller and moves very fast. Like Varroa, it chooses to raise its young in brood although the adult's mouthparts are not strong enough to penetrate the exoskeleton of adult bees. The damage is done to the brood with similar effects to Varroa; the deformed combs will help give away its presence. I mention it in the expectation that, inevitably, it will enter the UK. But it can be controlled by similar means to Varroa and beekeepers as always will rise to the challenge.

Small hive beetle (Aethina tumida)

This small black beetle has not yet been found in the UK. It tends to burrow into combs and can cause much damage to the brood inside; it does not prey on the brood or the adults but merely causes damage, like the wax moth. Recently imports of bees and bee products from countries where this pest has been found have been banned, but it may be only a matter of time before it reaches the UK.

CHAPTER 11

PREPARING FOR THE NEW SEASON

All too soon the season is over. Your bees have been well fed and provided for, they will have formed themselves into a loose group in the middle of their hive and will go into a state of dormancy – not true hibernation but almost. The queen, as ever, will be located at their centre and will perhaps lay just a few eggs each day. The colony will move around from outside to middle keeping everything warm and all will be silent.

For the beekeeper, however, there is no time to rest: there is much to do in order to greet the new season in a state of readiness. Preparation now will save much time and stress later.

In the hive, the new season will have begun as early as January. The queen will have started to lay a few eggs each day at first then gradually in increasing numbers; the winter bees will have begun to die and be replaced by the newly hatching brood, and at this stage the population of the hive may be at its lowest. Observe the hive on fine days and you may see a few flying bees – they will be looking for the first nectar and pollen, perhaps fetching water, all good signs, but it is too early to open the hive yet. If they have bee candy all will be well but resist the urge to start feeding them too early. The provision of food at this stage may induce the queen to start laying too soon in response to what the

hive perceives as a honey flow. When the resultant brood hatch there will be no nectar to fly to and the hive may starve. Let the season dictate the rate of progress and merely support your colony.

On the first day that it is warm enough to do so, when it seems mild and bees are flying in small numbers, carry out a very brief inspection and, at the least, change the floor, as it will be dirty after the long winter. Remove the floor to your work area and examine it for signs of disease; if it is littered with dead bees then action may be needed, since a healthy colony will remove the corpses as soon as the weather permits. The presence of dead bees need not be cause for alarm, but the fact that they have not removed them may be.

As soon as you are certain the bees are bringing in nectar and pollen, remove the bee candy and store it in the dry for next season. You will soon discover if this time has come by following the procedure below.

Locate a place in view of your hive, not too close to attract their attention and most certainly not in their flight line to and from the hive. Here you can place an old chair or, in my case, a number of empty hive boxes in which I kept a few hive tools and an old sack. On fine days when the bees have begun to fly, take yourself down to this spot (I use the

Healthy bees on hive front. (Courtesy Rupert Stephenson.)

sack to place on the boxes as a cushion), and just observe. You should notice quite a number of bees on the front of the hive and many more hovering up and down a few feet away. They will be orientating themselves on local landmarks and the sun ready to fly to forage later. Observe the bees returning – you will soon learn if they are returning filled with nectar, as they appear to make quite a heavy landing. It will be easier still to observe those returning with pollen, as the baskets on their back legs will be loaded, each with a small pill of compressed pollen. When pollen is being brought in it is a very good sign; the hive needs the pollen to feed brood and this should indicate that they are doing so. Observe the bees at the entrance – they may be just out of view inside the entrance hole but should greet each newcomer. They are not really being friendly, they are ascertaining if the visitor is a member of the club; if not, they will be ejected!

Just after noon, check the number of bees flying in and observe if there appears to be a queue for admission. If so, it may be time to replace your small winter entrance block for a larger one. They are fairly simple to make and I make a number of them, each with a progressively larger entrance slot. By watching the bees I like to enlarge the slot as they need it until, in the honey flow and much warmer weather, I remove it altogether. By this time the numbers in the hive will have increased sufficiently to supply enough entrance guards and unless I observe robbing by other bees, I leave it so until the honey flow has diminished. If you observe during the season you will notice that during the honey flow, when every bee is returning laden with produce, the bee will be permitted to enter any hive. As long as she is bringing in goods she will be allowed to enter; this is how 'drifting' occurs and can lead to spread of disease.

Spring flowers: it is time to open the enlarged entrance. (Courtesy Rupert Stephenson.)

It was during one of these observation periods many years ago that I saw bees returning laden with both nectar and pollen and they either misjudged the entrance or fell on landing. The bees then faced a long climb up the stand and the hive front before getting into the hive. Apart from the extra work it was causing many bees, I wanted my bees to be out foraging, not climbing the north face of the Eiger as it must seem to them. I immediately fabricated a stand with an alighting board attached, which was not fixed to the hive in any way so would not cause problems when I wanted to change brood boxes (*see* page 63). I noticed an immediate improvement: the bees had a larger target to aim for and the short walk up the sloping alighting board was simple compared to the previous experience (no bee ever missed the alighting board). I feel it was an improvement, and the fact that hive equipment manufacturers now sell such an item indicates many other beekeepers agree. With some simple tools and an accurate rule, you too can make your own; ordinary pine will suffice and it can be removed during the winter months. A beekeeping acquaintance here in France works 1,000 hives, every one of which has an alighting board.

As the season gets underway, the hive may decide it has enough pollen, which will have been stored in cells. When they consider the stores are sufficient you may well witness bees coming back out of the hive with their pollen baskets still attached, because they have been ordered out to gather nectar only (*see* page 14).

SPRING BUILD-UP

This is an important time for the hive and for you the observer. You may on fine spring days see many more bees flying to the flowers and returning laden with nectar and pollen; all seems well and you could be forgiven for assuming that all would remain so. However, we have a fickle climate in the UK and a period of fine weather can suddenly change. The hive has produced many more bees, there are many more emerging as a result of the flow of honey; then the weather turns around, it becomes dull and overcast, or very cold with late spring frosts, and the flowers stop producing nectar. The hive can manage for a while, as they have some stores to fall back on and are well used to this situation, but the extra number of eggs need feeding as grubs, and bees are emerging in ever greater numbers. It is frequently at this time that the hive begins to starve.

If you have not noticed soon enough, all is not lost: suit up, give them a little smoke and open up the hive. A quick inspection should confirm the worst; before you close up the hive, trickle a little sugar mixture along the top bars of the frames, just enough to keep them busy. Now make up a weak sugar solution and fit a half-gallon feeder over the crown board after removing the mesh.

It is important that this is a weak solution, say one part sugar dissolved in one part of warm water by volume. As distinct from winter feeding when we want as little water as possible in the hive so we make the solution as strong as we can, now we have no problem with water. However, if the sugar solution is too rich, the bees may prefer it to flying for nectar and remain inside while you feed them, for ever, a bit like teenagers!

This weak sugar solution will keep them alive but as soon as the weather turns once more, they will fly to the flowers and you can remove the feeder. You may also wish to add some proprietary pollen substitute and there is now on the market a cunning little feeder, plastic and easy to clean, which has two separate compartments, one for syrup and one for the dry pollen substitute. Bees have never had it so good but I would deny them nothing.

It is by your observation alone that this situation will be noticed and it may occur more than once before a long spell of reasonably settled weather comes and hopefully, with it, the main honey flow. A few simple actions, carried out in good time and costing very little, can make all the difference to a good season or a poor one, or between a good beekeeper and a bad one.

Monitoring your Varroa floors will soon indicate any sudden build-up of the pest and you should be able to take remedial steps before it becomes of epidemic proportions.

Out-apiary in woodland. (Courtesy J.C. Jeremy Hobson.)

CHAPTER 12
CONCLUSIONS

At the time of researching this book, the future of the honey bee looked, to me, rather bleak. Now, almost a year later, with worldwide concern and acceptance of the problem and recent substantial research being dedicated towards finding answers, I am filled with renewed hope and confidence.

What is certain is that *you* the beekeeper have much to contribute to the survival of the bee. While governments donate funds and research institutes labour long to discover answers, the amazing response from the beekeeping community has astounded many. The hive manufacturer who kindly donated some of the pictures for this book has reported their best trading year ever with demand for bees and equipment outstripping supply, a fact that fills me with great pleasure.

I stated at the start of this book that I wished to encourage the would-be beekeeper as I am firmly convinced that by increasing the number of colonies, and introducing new blood into the community of beekeepers, the welfare of the bee will be assured. The 'backyard' beekeeper has a great advantage over his commercial counterpart in that he has more time to devote per hive. By keeping bees in small units in urban environments he is protecting his bees from many of the agricultural sprays and practices thought to be contributory to the current situation, as the

French experience has demonstrated. There is no sight more rewarding than a super freshly filled with honey, especially when you consider the mass of flowering plants that have been pollinated to attain it.

I repeatedly come across the word 'stress' in researching disease. Whilst the practice has been carried out for many years, it must cause stress to the bee to be constantly moved from crop area to crop area for commercial gain (although it is not my aim to apportion blame, merely to explore theories). In the USA, it has long been the business of commercial beekeepers to transport their hives many hundreds of miles each season to the almond blossom in California; they receive a rental per hive for the bees during this period. Without the bees there would be no almond crop, which is a very important commercial enterprise on a very large scale.

The normally healthy bees may be resting during what is late winter in say, Montana, a northern state in America. The bees are awakened a few days and a few thousand miles later to find it is spring! Without the normal period of build-up, the hive now has to hurry into battle, to increase the colony to meet the sudden honey flow and to deal with this in days rather than the weeks it would have anticipated. This stress may be a contributory factor in triggering the latent

Freshly filled honey super; note the clean white cappings. (Courtesy The Food and Environment Research Agency, Crown Copyright.)

disease burden into epidemic proportion. On a smaller scale, throughout the world, where bees are being moved for this purpose, these stresses are exacerbating the burden of chemicals and diseases being carried by the honey bee, resulting in reported deaths.

Pollen is collected and sold for a similar purpose by beekeepers from many countries, and some of this pollen has been found to contain traces of over forty agricultural pesticides and fungicides.

Bees are being flown half way around the world in massive numbers to replace those lost through disease. When examined, the imported bees themselves carry IAPV, but it is only the stress of moving them that seems to trigger the disease into action.

The practice of importing bees and bee products from distant parts of the planet has proved to have serious consequences: with the bee comes disease, and our native bees do not have time to adapt to the new threat. This is a man-made problem and we will have to solve it, but what you can do is to provide a stable and benevolent environment

for your bees, on the small scale of our backyard 'planet'. We should aim not to 'import' bees or used items of bee equipment that have not been sterilized first, and likewise, we should not export them. Obtain a reliable strain of bees from a good source, ensure they are certified disease-free and try to keep them so. Good hygiene, regular brief inspections and efficient monitoring will help avoid any unwanted build-up of disease and mite infestation. Take steps immediately to deal with any problems, as procrastination over living creatures will surely result in dead creatures. Learn all you can and be prepared to be open minded and receptive to new ideas; be prepared to use and develop new treatments as they are discovered and by this means secure as large a population of them as you can (a Noah's Ark scenario). When the solutions are discovered, your bees can then go forward and re-populate the world. This is perhaps a romantic concept but what is certain is that, in keeping these wonderful creatures, and by patient observation, we can enjoy a wonderful pastime and somewhere out there a new beekeeper will look at his bees with fresh eyes and discover something that will advance the sum total of knowledge and help them to survive.

Beekeepers of my acquaintance are unlikely to give up because of the problems affecting their bees – sure, they will grumble about their misfortune and they will tell you they are giving up, but the next time you meet them, they will recount something they have read about to help their problem, or another fellow has passed on to them some advice which may help and so they continue. To the established beekeeper who may perhaps pick up this book I would say, 'Please, keep going, but most importantly, pass on what you have learned', as it is worth its weight in, well, at least honey!

There is evidence that the bees are helping themselves. Very early after Varroa had invaded these shores, strains of bees had been identified which could better cope with the pest. Some bees were more active in seeking out and destroying the mite; others bit the legs off the mite when discovered and were named 'leg biters' as a result and I am certain that out there somewhere more than a few wild strains have survived and have learned to manage. In the UK researchers are attempting to breed from strains displaying these good qualities.

The much-maligned Africanized bee has been found to be resistant to Varroa and other conditions affecting the bee. Unfortunately the bees will not survive in northern latitudes but researchers are racing to isolate the genes responsible for the resistance in order to incorporate them into our domestic stock.

In the meantime, we must not only help them to survive long enough for better treatments to be developed, but importantly to keep sufficient stocks active to pollinate the food crops. As mentioned on page 51, the Russian bee has displayed better management of Varroa. This is probably because this strain has been exposed to Varroa longer than any other and has developed ways to deal with it. However, in cross breeding it loses this ability, but the mere fact that some bees can manage is promising in itself. Surely it will be more beneficial both to man and the bee that a strain is developed that can manage disease better?

Unlike the popular media, with its tendency to exaggerate, the Food and Environmental Research Association site, Bee Base, will publish accurate and unemotional records of any disease or pest and often indicate ways to deal with them.

I may be forgiven for not including in Chapter 10 the possibility of woodpecker damage (in an urban environment it should not pose a problem); nor did I include the fact that in France this year large numbers of hornets caught and killed an astounding number of flying bees, or that France also suffers hive damage from wild boars. Moreover, in the northern states of America they have to protect hives from black bears, in Scotland sheep frequently rub against hives on the heather moors and push them over, and out-apiaries in the UK sometimes suffer loss and damage from wanton vandalism – where does one stop? If you were to consider every possible risk you would never get out of bed in the morning!

So all is far from lost and we have little to fear but fear itself; many beekeepers, including myself, look forward to the future as yet another challenge. Beekeeping periodicals constantly carry reports of progress and it is to that progress that I address this book, and to the future beekeepers I wish the very best of luck, because the future is very much in your hands.

GLOSSARY

Abdomen The third region of the body of the bee, containing the honey stomach, true stomach, intestine, sting and reproductive organs.

Absconding swarm A colony of bees that leaves the hive en masse because of disease or other maladies.

Adulterated honey Any product labelled as pure honey which contains a product other than honey.

Alighting board A small platform under the entrance of the hive.

American foul brood A brood disease of honey bees caused by the spore-forming bacterium, *Bacillus larvae*.

Anaphylactic shock Constriction of the muscles surrounding the bronchial tubes of a human, caused by hypersensitivity to venom and causing sudden death unless treated immediately.

Apiary Hives, colonies and other equipment in a location for the purposes of keeping bees.

Apiculture The science and craft of keeping bees.

Apis mellifera The scientific name of the honey bee.

Automatic uncapper An automated device that removes the capping from honeycomb prior to drawing off the honey.

Bacillus larvae The bacterium that causes American foul brood.

Bee bread A name sometimes used for the mixture of pollen and honey stored as food for the colony.

Bee brush A soft brush used to remove bees from the combs or other areas of the hive.

Bee candy A solid block of sugar given to bees to assist them in times of starvation or for supplementing winter feeding.

Bee dance A series of vigorous dancing movements within the hive by a returning field bee to inform other workers of the direction and intensity of food she has visited.

Bee escape A one-way valve used to clear bees from an area of the hive.

Bee space The space left between combs which is too large to fill with propolis and too small to block with brace comb.

Bee substance The substance exuded by a fecund and active queen, which reassures the members of her hive that all is well.

Bee veil A cloth or wire mesh sheet used for protecting the head area of the beekeeper.

Bee venom The substance injected into the victim by the bee.

Beehive The box fitted with removable frames and used for housing a colony of bees.

Beeswax The wax produced by the bee from slits in the abdomen and used for building comb.

Bottom board Another name for the floor of the hive.

Brace comb Construction of odd pieces of wax comb built between areas greater than the bee space.

Braula coeca The scientific name for a wingless fly known as the bee louse.

Brood   Bees in the comb as eggs, larvae or pupae and not yet emerged from their cells.

Brood chamber   The area in the hive where brood are raised.

Capped brood   Also called 'sealed brood', developing bees whose cells have been sealed over with wax.

Cappings   The wax cap from honey-filled comb after it has been removed for extraction.

Cell   The wax compartment in a honeycomb.

Chilled brood   Immature bees that have died from exposure to cold.

Chunk honey   Honey cut from frames with the comb and placed in jars of liquid honey.

Clarifying   Removing visible particles from drawn honey or settling to remove air bubbles.

Clearer board   A device of various design used to permit bees to pass through but not return, permitting the beekeeper to clear all the bees from, for example, the honey supers.

Cluster   A group of bees hanging together as in a clustered swarm on a branch.

Colony   A collection of bees with workers, drones and brood attending a laying queen.

Comb   The assembly of hexagonal wax cells, in two tiers joined at the bases and used for the storage of honey, pollen and propolis and the rearing of brood.

Comb foundation   Commercially produced sheets of wax, sometimes wired for strength and embossed with the shape of the cells on both sides.

Comb honey   Honey sold with the comb, either cut from frames or produced in thin wooden sections.

Corbicular loads   Name given to the small pellets of compressed pollen carried in the hair 'baskets' on the rear legs of the honey bee.

Creamed honey   Honey that has started to crystallize and subsequently is beaten to a creamy consistency.

Crown board   Board made to the size of the hive that covers the topmost box under the roof. Constructed with two apertures suitable for the insertion of Porter bee escapes, this can double as a clearer board.

Decoy hive   A hive placed to attract stray swarms.

De-queen   To remove the queen from a colony.

Dividing   Separating a colony to form two or more parts.

Double brood box   A means of increasing the brood area available by adding a second brood box above the first.

Drawn combs   Combs that have had the cells built out from the foundation sheet.

Drifting   The failure of bees to return to their own colony in an apiary.

Drone   The male honey bee.

Drone comb   Larger cells for the purpose of raising drones.

Drone layer   An infertile worker bee that lays eggs which only produce drones, sometimes called a laying worker.

Dysentery   The condition affecting bees with Nosema (and sometimes starvation), resulting in diarrhoea.

European foul brood   An infectious brood disease of honey bees.

Eke   Usually used to describe an extra spacer placed in a hive to accommodate a feeder; may also refer to thin strips of foundation fitted in frames to act as a starter.

Extracted honey   Honey removed from the comb by centrifugal force.

Fermentation   The chemical breakdown of honey associated with a high moisture content.

Fertile queen   A queen that has mated naturally with a drone or has been artificially inseminated and can lay fertilized eggs.

Field bees   Worker bees that fly to collect nectar and pollen for the hive.

Food chamber   A hive body filled with honey and pollen to provide winter stores.

Foundation   Purified and moulded sheets of beeswax, sometimes wired for strength and imprinted with the shape of the cells.

Frame   A wooden construction consisting of a top bar, two end bars and either a one-piece or two-piece bottom bar to contain the comb.

Granulation   Another name for the crystallization of honey.

Haemolymph   A clear fluid that circulates through the bee in the same manner as blood does in other animals.

Hive block   A strip of wood designed to partially or completely close the entrance to the hive and may be enlarged as the season progresses.

Hive body   Sometimes called a brood body, designed to hold the brood area of a hive.

Hive stand   The structure that supports the hive may be wooden, brick or made from other materials.

Hive tool   A device of varying design used to pry up the frames and scrape wax and propolis from the hive parts.

Honey   A sweet viscous material comprising sugars, produced by the bee from the nectar of flowers.

Honeydew   A sweet liquid excreted by aphids that is sometimes collected by bees in the absence of flower nectar (it does not make good honey).

Honey extractor   A machine that extracts the honey from frames of uncapped comb by centrifugal force.

Honey flow   The periods when nectar is plentiful and bees can collect and store honey.

Honey gate   A valve or tap used to draw honey from an extractor or storage bin.

Honey stomach   An organ in the abdomen of the bee, separate from its normal stomach and used for carrying nectar, honey or water.

Larva (pl. larvae)   The second stage of bee metamorphosis; a white, legless grub.

Laying worker   A worker that lays infertile eggs, producing only drones (usually in response to a hive that is queen-less).

Manipulating cloths   Stout cloths filled with timber or plastic strips at each end, used in pairs to partially and progressively cover the top of the hive while manipulating to avoid stress to the bees.

Mating flight   The flight taken by a virgin queen while she mates with several drones.

Mead   Wine made from honey.

Melittiphis   Small mite that lives on honey and pollen but does not harm the bee.

Migratory beekeeping   The practice of moving colonies of bees from one area to another to take advantage of honey flows.

Nazenov gland   A gland at the base of the bee's thorax on the upper side which emits a strong scent that will attract other bees.

Nectar   A sweet liquid secreted by the nectaries of flowers to attract bees and from which honey is made.

Nosema   A disease of adult honey bees caused by *Nosema apis*.

Nucleus   A small colony of bees, usually covering two to five frames, sometimes called a 'nuc' and used to start a new hive.

Nurse bees   Bees three to ten days old which look after the developing brood.

Observation hive   A hive fitted with one or more walls of glass or clear plastic to allow observation of bees at work.

Orientation flight   The short flights taken

by young bees in front of the hive to orientate themselves with their location.

Out-apiary An apiary located away from the home of the beekeeper.

Paralysis A viral disease of adult bees affecting their limbs or wings.

Parthenogenesis The development of drones from unfertilized eggs.

Piping The sounds made by an emerging queen as she hatches.

Pollen The male reproductive cells produced by the anthers of flowers; high in protein, they are collected by bees and taken back to be stored as food.

Pollen basket A flattened area on the outside of the bee's hind legs surrounded by stiff hairs in which the bee collects pollen and propolis for transport back to the hive.

Pollen substitute Commercially produced material, usually of vegetable origin, which can be fed to bees in the spring to stimulate brood rearing.

Pollen trap A device that can be fitted to hives to collect pollen grains as the bee enters.

Pollination The transfer of pollen from the anthers to the stigma of flowering plants.

Pollinator The agent responsible for transfer of pollen from the anther to the stigma of flowering plants, commonly bees, flies and beetles.

Prime swarm The first swarm to leave the parent colony, usually with the old queen.

Proboscis The mouth parts of the bees, which are formed into a sucking tube or tongue.

Propolis Compounds of a sticky nature collected by bees for repairing cracks in the hive, usually from tree saps and other similar sources.

Pupa (pl. pupae) The third stage of development of the honey bee during which the adult bee organs are formed.

Queen A fully developed female bee, the queen is longer and larger than a worker bee.

Queen cage A small cage in which a queen and a number of workers may be confined for transport or to introduce into a hive to be re-queened.

Queen cell A special elongated cell, larger than a worker or drone cell, in which queens are raised.

Queen clipping The practice of clipping part of one or both wings of a queen to prevent her from flying.

Queen cup A man-made cup of wax or plastic, inserted into the hive to induce the bees to complete it and raise a queen.

Queen excluder A device consisting either of metal bars or perforated sheet, designed to permit access by worker bees but restrict the drones and queen to other areas of the hive.

Queen substance The pheromone secreted by glands in the queen bee and moved throughout the colony by the workers to reassure others of the queen's presence.

Rendering wax The processes of melting down surplus wax from cappings or old comb for re-use.

Robbing The stealing of nectar or honey by bees from other colonies.

Royal jelly A highly nutritious glandular secretion of young bees used to feed the queen and raise young brood.

Sac brood A disease of brood caused by a virus.

Scout bees Worker bees searching for new sources of nectar or pollen or searching for a new location to house a swarm.

Sealed brood *See* 'Capped brood'.

Self-spacing frames Frames constructed so they are a bee space apart when fitted together in a hive.

Shaken swarm Method of transferring a

colony of bees from a diseased hive into a clean one, for example to remedy European foul brood.

Skep Hive made from twisted straw and without internal moveable frames.

Smoker A device in which sacking, cardboard or other flammable materials are burnt to produce smoke.

Solar wax extractor A glass-covered insulated box that utilizes the rays of the sun to render down used wax.

Spermatheca A special organ of the queen in which she stores sperm from her mating.

Sting The modified ovipositor of the bee used as a weapon of defence.

Super Any brood body or special shallow body used for the storage of honey.

Supersedure A natural replacement of an established queen by one of her daughters.

Swarm The mass of bees (including the queen) that exits the hive en masse to start another colony.

Swarming The natural method of reproduction for the honey bee.

Trickle method A process of running a liquid along the frame tops, either of sugar syrup to give immediate aid to a starving colony, or to apply liquid medication.

Uncapping knife The knife used to remove cappings from a comb of sealed honey prior to removing the honey.

Venom allergy A condition in which a person receiving a sting will react with anything from a mild rash or swelling to anaphylactic shock. Such a person should consult a doctor before handling bees.

Venom hypersensitivity A condition in which a person if stung is likely to experience anaphylactic shock. People with this known sensitivity should carry an emergency syringe of cortisone at all times.

Virgin queen An unmated queen.

Wax glands The eight glands on the last four segments of a bee's abdomen that secrete wax.

Wax moth Larvae of the moth *Golleria mellonclia*, which seriously damages brood and empty combs.

Winter cluster The name for the bee's tight ball-like formation adopted for warmth and protection during the winter months.

Worker bee A female bee that has undeveloped reproductive organs. These form the largest population in the hive and as the name suggests do most of the work!

Worker comb The most frequently observed comb in which workers are raised.

FURTHER INFORMATION

PUBLICATIONS

de Bruyn, Clive, *Practical Beekeeping* (Crowood Press, 1997).

Snelgrove, L.E., *Swarming: Its Control and Prevention* (Snelgrove and Smith, 1981).

Waring, Claire (ed.), *Bee Craft* magazine. Stoneycroft, Back Lane, Little Addington, Kettering, Northamptonshire NN14 4AX.

WEBSITES

To view the images on the excellent BeeBase website go to:

https://secure.fera.defra.gov.uk/beebase/ and click on 'Image Gallery'. For your local bee inspector go to the 'Contacts Page' and enter your postcode.

For the latest information on threats of Tropilaelaps and small hive beetle in the UK, go to: https://secure.fera.defra.gov.uk/beebase/index.cfm?pageid=92.

INDEX